Water Bath Canning and Preserving Cookbook

A Beginners Guide for Learning How to Can and Preserve Food in Jars such as Pickled Vegetables, Jams, Jellies, etc. with Tested Homemade Recipes

By

Fiona Begum

Disclaimer

This publication is designed to provide competent and reliable information regarding the subject matter covered. However, the views expressed in this publication are those of the author alone, and should not be taken as expert instruction or professional advice. The reader is responsible for his or her own actions.

The author hereby disclaims any responsibility or liability whatsoever that is incurred from the use or application of the contents of this publication by the purchaser or reader. The purchaser or reader is hereby responsible for his or her own actions.

Table of Contents

Introduction

Water bath canning, also known as boiling water bath, is a simple way of preserving homemade pickles, tomato sauce, fruits, jams and acidic foods in general in jars through a process called canning.

You may want to ask why water bath canning instead of pressure canning. Although preservative methods are safe for home canning, there are several reasons you should use water bath canning instead of pressure canning. Still, if the homemade food you want to preserve is acidic, such as pickled vegetables, jams, fruits and tomato sauce, your best bet is to use the water bath canning technique. The temperature created through pressure canning is above the required temperature for water bath canning, which is why acidic foods processed through water bath canning retain their fresh flavor throughout the year.

If you're new to water bath canning and wondering how to get started, this book, *Water Bath Canning and Preserving Cookbook*, will help take you through everything you need to know about canning and preserving food in jars.

With water bath canning, you are assured of a fresh flavored supply of preserved acidic foods that can be processed easily for little to no cost and with no special skills or equipment required.

Chapter 1

Water Bath Canning Basics

Why Water Bath Canning?

Water bath canning is mainly for food with high acidic levels, such as fruits, jams, salsas, jellies, pickled vegetables, tomatoes, berries, and sauerkraut. The acidic level, combined with the required time for a water bath to boil, enables the safe preservation of the food without high pressure, as in the case of pressure canners. In essence, you pack your food into heated, disinfected Mason jars and submerge them for a certain period of time in a pot of boiling hot water. Boiling water helps preserve food with a shelf life that spans months or even years by destroying any bacteria that could cause it to decay, sucking air out from the jar and, helping the lid to latch onto the jar, sealing firmly.

Water bath canning is not advisable for food with low acidic levels, such as chili, poultry, seafood, beans, meats, and some vegetables, which need a high temperature of up to 116° C (240° F) to increase the heat inside the jars not less than 100°C (212° F) – the boiling point of water and heated to the capacity of exterminating all toxic bacteria. Instead of water bath canning food with low acidic levels, you should pressure can them.

Is Water Bath Canning Safe?

The safety of foods preserved in a hot water bath canner is guaranteed, provided the jars are sealed appropriately, and the recipes used are not for pressure canners but water bath canners.

Preservation through water bath canning is mainly for foods with high acidic levels, as earlier mentioned. Do not process vegetables (except pickled) and meats through water bath canning, but through pressure canning which can subject the foods to high enough temperature to destroy the toxic bacteria.

Fruits contain high acid levels and are suitable for water bath canning. The acid level in foods is an important criterion for selecting the method of home preservation to be used, as acids curb the development of bacteria that can lead to botulism which thrive in home canned foods.

The acidic level of tomatoes is in-between sufficiently safe for water bath canning and insufficiently safe. There is a vast difference in the natural acid level of tomatoes, which necessitates the inclusion of lemon juice, vinegar, and citric acid to enhance the acid level of tomatoes, making them safe after canning.

Water Bath Canning Foods You Can Safely Preserve

Not all foods can be water bath canned, and not all can be pressure canned. This can be confusing, especially for beginners. It is simpler to understand and utilize water bath canning for preserving foods. Here is a list of twenty-one foods that you can safely can using the water bath method.

- **Apple Butter**

Many people use the water bath method to can apple butter for different reasons. For the making of applesauce, apple butter is required. You can use a canning or crock pot to can apple butter.

- **Applesauce**

Applesauce can easily be made; all it requires is chopping the apples and making your applesauce.

- **BBQ Sauce**

BBQ sauce is safe when water bath canned, just like tomato sauce. Your grilled meat, and homemade splash, are all safe.

- **Berries**

The acid level of berries is high, making them suitable for water bath canning. You can preserve berries such as huckleberries, blackberries, raspberries, elderberries, and blueberries.

- **Cranberry Sauce**

Cranberry sauce is another food safe for water bath canning.

- **Juice**

Juice is safe for water bath canning. Instead of going through the stress of making juice all the time, you can produce your juice and preserve it, and the flavor is retained throughout the year. Apple juice, berry juice, orange juice, grape juice, tomato juice, etc., are safe for canning.

- **Peaches**

Peaches can be halved or sliced with the addition of half water or juice. Another option you can add to peaches when canning is sugar syrup. It is advised to use a canning pot with a rack for your canning, even though a large pot can be improvised for water bath canning.

- **Plums**

Plums are also safe for water bath canning. These fruits can be canned using the water bath method due to their high acidic level and sugar volume.

Other foods that can be canned using the water bath method include:

- Tomatoes

- Pickles such as cucumbers, beans, zucchini, and radishes.

- Relishes

- Ketchup

- Pears

- Tomato salsa

- Cherries

- Pie fillings such as peach, cherry, apple, blueberry, etc.

- Water

- Fruit jam

- Jellies such as fruit, flower, or vegetables

- Fruit preserves

- Tomato sauce

- Vinaigrette dressings

Foods Not Safe To Can At All

As earlier said, not all foods are safe for water bath canning due to their inability to eliminate toxic microorganisms and interference with the process of heat transfer, thereby enabling the survival of bacteria. With the exclusion of foods meant to be pressured canned, here is a list of foods that should not be canned **AT ALL**, and this is also applicable to pressure canning.

The procedures for canning some food products are available on the internet. However, caution should be taken in ensuring they are from reliable sources such as the National Center for Home Food Preservation, USDA guide to home canning, and Cooperative Extension websites in states across the US.

- **Pasta and Rice**

Foods like pasta, noodles, and rice are not to be put in canned products because of starch interference with heat transfer to the center of the jar. You can only serve a chicken broth or spaghetti sauce with your freshly cooked noodles, rice, or pasta.

- **Dairy Products**

The best form of preservation for dairy products is freezing. Water bath canning, atmospheric steaming, or pressure canning should never be used for dairy products. Due to the low acid level of dairy products, they enable the development of a harmful bacteria known as Clostridium botulinum which develops spores when stored at room temperature.

The use of dairy products in some canned recipes like pasta and cheese, meat gravy, custard pot filling mixes, and creamed soups should be strictly avoided. Freezing them or preparing them from scratch is rather advised.

- **Bread and Cakes in a Jar**

Once you remove your baked bread and cakes in glass jars that are sealed with lids, they are no longer safe for consumption because Clostridium botulinum can grow in them due to their low acidic level; this can lead to food poisoning.

It is not advisable to bake in canning jars because they can be destroyed in the oven by dry heat.

- **Butter, Cheese, and Milk**

Take note that butter, cheese, and milk should not be canned. Even though some online sources classify them as suitable for canning, they should not be canned. If you pour dissolved butter into a jar, seal the lid and refrigerate to a solid state – heat is excluded in this process. The absence of heat makes the process unsafe for room temperature storage. Although some sources suggest heating cheese or butter in a dry oven, no research backs up the safety of this process. Before the harmful bacteria can be destroyed and the seal adequately sealed, the heat has to attain a certain temperature. The jars could get broken before this temperature is attained, and you may sustain an injury. The same applies to cheese; they retain water in high proportion, enabling the development of harmful bacteria. Avoid using any dairy products for recipes intended for canning.

- **Oil**

Placing oil coats in food or herbs can result in the growth of Clostridium botulinum. Do not seal fresh vegetables, fruits, or herbs; put oil in a jar or bottle for storage at room temperature.

Other foods that are not safe to be canned at all include:

- Pickled eggs

- Starch

  Very dense purees such as winter squash, cooked dried beans, mashed pumpkin, mashed potatoes, etc.

- Tender food products

- Other products such as cauliflower, summer squash, Broccoli, eggplant, cabbage, lettuce, sweets, grains, lard, cornstarch and flour, and nuts

Rules for Safe Water Bath Canning

1. Start With The Best Produce

The number one rule for water bath canning is selecting the best produce. If you're preserving vegetables or fruits, ensure you settle for products of the best quality (fresh and ripe), and avoid using products that are damaged or overripe so that your end product after the water bath canning will be top-notch quality.

If the product quality is bad, you may end up with bad products that won't stand the storage duration. Good quality produce ensures all round safety all through the storage season.

2. Observe The Recipe Closely

Certified recipes for water bath canning have been thoroughly researched and tested to guarantee the maintenance of acidic levels throughout the stipulated storage duration. That is why you must comply with all stated procedures in the recipe to avoid deviation from the acidic level, which can result in spoilage or non-safety of your processed food.

Avoid adjusting the quantity of the ingredients for safety reasons. For instance, do not be tempted to use three teaspoons if the recipe states two teaspoons. Some recipe ingredients such as garlic can reduce the pH level of your food, rendering it unsafe for water bath canning. Even if you prefer extra garlic for taste or flavor, do not include it before processing your food but when you serve it. Mastering the water bath canning technique should not stop you from abiding by the recipe.

3. Make Your Working Area Ready

Water bath canning is not rocket science. Nonetheless, the process comprises two parts; the preparation of food and the preservation of food. The first part involves the required work to be done before the beginning of the water bath canning process, like cutting fruits or vegetables to the desired size and cooking sauces and jams.

To simplify the process and keep you composed, ensure to assemble all necessary equipment and ingredients in a tidy kitchen. Read and understand the recipes to know what is required before you begin the water bath canning. If a piece of particular equipment is needed, like a food mill, ensure it is in place before proceeding.

4. Only High Acidic Foods Should Be Water Bath Canned

Another important rule for water bath canning is to only can foods with high acid levels, which have already been over-flogged.

Acidity is a critical factor when canning because harmful bacteria that can cause botulism cannot develop in places with high acid levels (environments where the pH level is not more than 4.6).

Food products with low acid levels such as poultry, soups, seafood, red meat, stock, and vegetables (carrots, pumpkins, potatoes, green beans, etc.) require pressure canning to be safe for consumption and storage.

5. Use New Lids Constantly

For canning, Mason jars (glass) are reusable. However, ensure you constantly inspect the jars for cracks and dents. It is important to also clean the jars with soap and water (hot) and disinfect them thoroughly before filling them up with the food products you want to can.

The metal rings latching the lid onto the jars called bands are also reusable, provided they are thoroughly washed before use. However, it would be best if you used new lids when canning. When a lid is latched onto a jar, it loses its compactness and is not as strong as before. If the lids are reused, the jars' sealing will not be firm, leading to food spoilage.

After securing a variety of Mason jars, adding a few lids to your collections can be beneficial in the long run.

Always withdraw the bands from your jars before storing all water bath canned food products, which help reveal possible problems such as improperly sealed jars, the development of bacteria on the lid of improperly sealed jars, and food spoilage. The standard practice is removing the bands after completing your water bath canning. The safety of your water bath canned food products should always be a priority.

6. Ensure The Safety Of The Storage Of Your Food And Arrange it Properly

The final rule for water bath canning is to ensure the safety and quality of your water bath canned food. This is vital for storing your food, irrespective of the preservation method. After completing the water bath canning of your food, seal the lids, and allow the jars to cool off for at least 12 hours before attempting to remove them from the cooling place.

It is important to properly label and date your jars before storage. For storing your jars, it is best to store them in cool and dark places where sunlight or direct heat cannot penetrate. Ensure the temperature is stable (do not increase or decrease lower than 23°C or 75°F).

When arranging your jars, ensure you do not pile them on each other to prevent cracks and breaks. If stacking jars is required, ensure you only stack jars of the lesser weights or at most the same weight on each other, and do not place heavy jars on lighter ones.

For the arrangement of your canned foods, do it accordingly. Place newly canned food jars at the back and shift the former canned food jars to the front. This is to avoid using up new jars and later discovering old expired or spoilt jars due to poor arrangement.

The standard duration for storing water bath canned food jars is twelve months. However, the stored food may last longer than that, but it is advisable not to store your food for more than a year. Ensure to make use of your canned foods in good time. If you have canned food that you have stored for more than a year, and you are not sure of its safety, it is advisable you dispose of them rather than eat contaminated food.

Chapter 2

Canning Glossary of Terms

Acetic Acid

This is the main acid in vinegar, which is a strong, transparent liquid (vinegar is 5 percent acetic acid). Vinegar is sour because of acetic acid.

Ascorbic Acid

This is the scientific term for vitamin C, a soluble vitamin found in nature and is sold to the public as white, odorless powder or crystals. It serves as an antioxidant to prevent oxidation and keep fruits and vegetables that are light-colored from browning.

Altitude

The upward height (distance in feet or meters) of an area above ocean level.

Counterfeit Sugar

Any of many artificially delivered non-nutritive sweet substances. Counterfeit sugars change in pleasantness yet are typically ordinarily better than granulated sugar.

Bacteria

There are microscopic organisms that can be hazardous and are present in the soil, water, and air surrounding. Some bacteria produce poisons that must be eliminated by heating to 240°F (116°C) for a predetermined period of time because they flourish in preserved foods that are low in acids. Low-acid foods must therefore be canned in a pressure canner.

Botulism

Food poisoning brought on by consuming poisons caused by the bacteria Clostridium botulinum. Botulism may result in death. The spores of this bacteria are typically found in the soil, wind, and dust that clings to raw food. They are a member of a group of bacteria incapable of growing in the presence of air and typically do not flourish in foods high in acidity. Any firmly closed jar of low-acid food yet to undergo the proper processing can support the growth of the spores. Toxin-producing spores can be eliminated by processing low-acid foods at the proper temperature and length of time.

Band

The canning ring tightens and adheres round the bands to prevent the lid from falling off during processing.

Headspace

The unfilled space in a crisp protecting container between the highest point of the food or fluid and the underside of the cover. The right measure of headspace is fundamental to consider food extension as the containers are warmed and to develop a solid vacuum seal as containers cool.

Canner

One of two items of equipment used in fresh preservation to process jars with food products inside and enclosed with two-piece lids on top. Boiling water canners for high-acid foods and pressure canners for low-acid foods are the two canner types suggested for use while preserving fresh foods

Citrus Acid

An organic acid that comes from citrus fruits like lemons and limes. It is offered as white crystals or granules. It is a component of commercial produce protectors that prevents oxidation, as well as pectin products that help gel formation by raising the acidity of jam or jelly.

Fresh Preservation

This is when fresh produce and freshly made foods are preserved in glass jars with lids and bands using heat to eliminate the microorganisms responsible for spoilage. This terminology is also used to describe home canning.

Brine

A saltwater mixture used for pickling or food preservation. While sugar and spices are occasionally added, salt and water are the primary ingredients.

Pectin

A carbohydrate that normally exists in fruits and vegetables. As fruits and vegetables become ripe, the content of the pectin reduces. Therefore, they get soft and their form becomes lost. Pectin is commercially sold both in the liquid and powder forms and can be used in making jellies, jams, and other spreads that are soft.

Pickling

For food preservation, particularly vegetables and cucumbers, in a vinegar acidic mixture (mostly with spices included to give it some flavor). Boiiling water canners are used to process pickled foods.

Spice Bag

A little muslin bag that holds the entire spices and herbs while you cook. The bag enables the spices and herb's flavor to permeate the food, and also making it easy for the spices to be removed when you are done cooking. In the absence of a spice bag, the spices and herbs can be tied in a square of cheesecloth.

Cheesecloth

A lightweight, woven cloth with multiple applications in the kitchen. It can be shaped into a bag to keep whole herbs and spices while cooking, making removal easier. For fresh preservation, it can replace a jelly bag to separate juice from fruit pulp while producing jelly or homemade juice.

Canning Salt

This salt is frequently used to improve the taste of canned foods and is suggested for food preservation.

Bubble Remover

A non-metallic tool used to release or expel air bubbles that have become trapped inside jars during fresh preservation. Air bubbles must be expelled before using the two-piece closure to maintain adequate headspace.

Microorganism

A minuscule living organism, such as mold, yeast, or bacteria that can contaminate frozen or preserved goods.

Home Canning

This involves employing heat processing to eliminate bacteria that cause rot so as to preserve freshly prepared foods in glass jars with two-piece closures.

Hot-Pack Technique

This involves putting hot, preheated food into jars before they are heat-processed in a canner. Food that has been preheated releases extra air, enables a tighter pack in the jar, and lessens floating. When it comes to hard foods, this method is recommended over the raw-pack technique.

Raw-Pack Technique

Putting raw, unheated food into jars before heating it

Mason Jar

A glass jar that is very appropriate for boiling water or pressure canning heat-processed foods and/or liquids. Mason jars are made to resist the high temperatures and repeated use involved in fresh preservation. True mason jars also adhere to a set of dimensions and weights in line with approved safe heat processing procedures. The jars come in sizes ranging from 4 ounces (125 mL) to 1 quart.

Heat Processing or Processing

To altogether remove enzymes and eliminate dangerous molds, yeasts, and bacteria, food must be heated to a specific temperature and for a specific amount of time in filled jars. All foods that are home-preserved require heat processing to maintain food safety. Bacteria that are inherently present in food and/or enter the jar during filling are destroyed during processing. It also enables gases or air to be expelled from the jar to produce an airtight vacuum seal as the food cools, eliminating food recontamination.

Process Time

The period of time full jars are heated in a pressure canner or boiling water canner. The processing time has to be adequate to heat the coolest area in the jar. Every contemporary, tested fresh recipe includes a processing time that is dependent on various variables like acidity, food product type, and jar size.

Chapter 3

Getting Started With Water Bath Canning

Tools and Supplies for Water Bath Canning

Getting started with water bath canning requires having some important supplies that will make your canning process easy. Even though you may minimize the cost of some items, the safety and quality of your processed food should be your topmost priority. Below is a list of supplies needed to get started with water bath canning.

Boiling Water Canner

Boiling water canners are big deep pots typically made of aluminum with matched lids and ample depth to entirely immerse the jars with a residual space of an inch above the jar's tops. It is best to use flat bottoms when working on cooktops.

Rack

It is important to have a rack that matches the inner part of the canner to maintain a safe distance between the jars and the direct heat from the base of the stockpot, which prevents the jars from being placed directly on the base of your canner; thus preventing heat from cracking the jars.

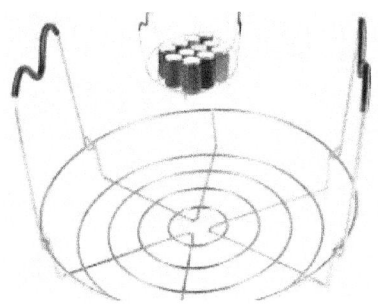

Canning Jars

Kerr, Mason, or Bell mainly manufacture canning jars. They vary in size ranging from 4 oz.-quarts of wide-mouthed and narrow-mouthed variants. The jars are often reusable.

Note: Do not use recycled pickle and mayonnaise, ornamental glass storage jars, old-fashioned canning jars, and lids sealed with rubber jars.

Metal Bands

The metal bands tighten the rims of the jars and fasten the lids throughout the processing, sealing, and cooling time. Ensure they are clean, rust-free, and undamaged or without dents. They are also reusable.

Metal Canning Lids

The lids are important when canning; new canning lids should be used every time you can. They should never be reused. They are built with an internal gasket that loses up due to heat during processing, enabling air to pass through the jar when cooling, then becoming airtight after cooling the jars.

Canning Funnel

Canning funnels, mainly plastic made or stainless steel, ensure food does not spill onto the jar rims when filling them up due to their wide mouth.

Ladle

Ladles are usually stainless steel made. If replacing your ladle, ensure you get a design with a long handle with a pouring rim or sprout.

Jar Lifter

Jar lifters are specially fitted tongs around the bottom of the canning jar's rims for the safe gripping and lifting of hot jars in and out of the canner after processing and to drop off the jars in a canner of boiling water.

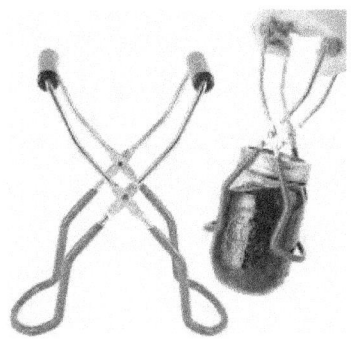

Bubble Remover

You can get a real tool that you can slip into your full jars to get rid of bubbles. I merely use a chopstick or a plastic knife.

Strainer or Food Mill

They are of different sizes and designs, usually good for crushing soft, cooked foods and for sieving them such that the skins and seeds can be removed from the pulp.

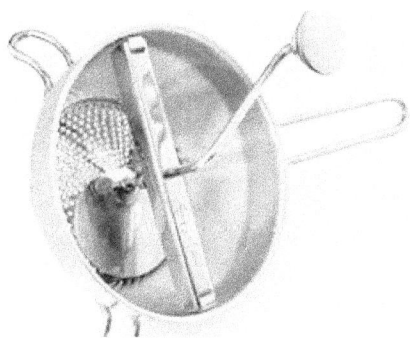

Stockpot

Use stainless steel stock pots big enough for holding and cooking big portions of food products like berries, tomatoes, etc., before scooping them into your jars for processing inside the canners.

Cooking Surface

Your cooking surface is very important, do not use an oven, dishwasher, or microwave for your canning as this is highly unsafe; use a gas or an electric stovetop.

Step-By-Step Water Bath Canning Process

You must arrange the equipment, supplies, and work area and get yourself ready before you start the canning. Strictly use tested recipes certified for canning foods only in a water bath canner.

1. **Review The List of Ingredients**

- Ensure you go through the ingredient lists, confirming the required quantity of each ingredient in the recipe.

2. **Prepare Your Jars and Lids**

- Inspect your jars if there are leaks, uneven rims, and cracks before you begin canning. Ensure to inspect the lids for scratches, missing seals, or unevenness. Also, check if the ring bands are fitted with the jars.

- The jars, ring bands, and lids should be cleaned in soapy water (hot), rinsed thoroughly, and drained. Decontaminate the jars if the processing will not be up to ten minutes by covering the jars inside boiling water for at least ten minutes. Decontamination is not required if the jars will be processed for more than ten minutes.

- Keep the jars filled with hot prepared food products inside the water of 83°C (180°F) to heat the jars before filling them up. This can be done in another pan or the canner. Alternatively, you can wash the jars in a dishwasher and monitor when to bring them out when you are prepared to use them. The lids of the jars may be heated or not.

3. **Prepare The Hot Water Canner**

- The rack should be placed at the base of the canner.

- Pour water into the canner (not less than half of the canner).

- Close the canner and heat up to a temperature of 60°C (140°F) for raw foods and 83°C (180°F) for hot packed foods.

- Prepare another hot water in another pan that will be used to fill up the canner later.

4. Prepare The Food

The preparation steps are dependent on the procedures stated in the recipe and the type of food you want to can.

- Avoid double recipe per time, only prepare a canner load capacity per time.

- Carefully arrange the items based on their size and quality, and set aside bad products.

- Thoroughly wash your produce in clean cold water, and drain them in a colander well enough.

- Utilize a raw or hot pack based on recipe procedures.

- Bright-colored fruits should be kept in a solution of ascorbic acid or a color preservative to avoid losing color.

- Make a sugar syrup if you are canning fruits. Although fruits can be canned without sugar syrup, the fruits will lose most of their firmness and not retain their color.

- Acidify Asian Pears, Figs, and Tomatoes with:

  - One tablespoon of bottled lemon juice (per pint jar) or 2 tablespoons per quart jar.

  - ¼ teaspoon of citric acid per pint jar or ½ teaspoon per quart jar; alternatively, you can use Vinegar instead of citric acid. 2 tablespoons of Vinegar per pint jar or ¼ cup per quart jar (this may affect the flavor).

- Ensure you use sufficient Vinegar for pickles and relishes. Do not decrease the quantity.

- For salsa, ensure you use a certified recipe with sufficient lime, lemon juice, or Vinegar to curb the growth of microbes.

- Process the jellies and jams for five minutes if the jars are uncontaminated and ten minutes if not.

- Use low or no sugar-required pectin if you are canning a reduced sugar jam or jelly. Processing these may take longer to process, strictly flow recipe procedures.

5. Fill The Jars

- Drain off water from the hot jars, fill up with food products, and seal per time. Insert the filled-up jar into the hot canner until done.

- Use appropriate headspace: headspace of half an inch is used when canning most fruits, relishes, pickles, and a quarter inch for jellies and jams.

- Use a plastic knife or bubble freer to remove air bubbles in the jars.

- Clean the rims of the jars using a kitchen cloth.

- Put a lid on the jar.

- Place and tighten the ring band firmly.

6. Fill The Canners

- Put the filled-up and sealed jars into the canner using a jar lifter. Avoid jars wedging against each other.

- Ensure the water level is not less than an inch from the top of the jar; adjust if necessary by adding water until sufficient.

7. Process Your Canner

- Heat the canner at a high temperature. Time the processing from the point the canner starts boiling. Follow the recipe's stated time, set your timer, and adjust the altitude as required.

- If the boiling is halted during the processing, start the process from scratch.

8. Cooling Time

- After turning off the heat, remove your canner from the burner when safe, remove the canner's cover and let the jars remain in the water for at least five minutes.

9. Removing Your Jars

- Get the counter ready for the jars by placing a twofold layer of kitchen towels on it off the drafts or using cutting boards.

- Ensure the jars are leveled by removing them with a jar lifter and placing them on the prepared counter. You can use a dry towel to support the jar.

- Maintain a distance not less than an inch for proper air circulation around the jars, and avoid retightening the ring bands.

10. Jars Storage

- When storing the jars, remove the ring bands after cooling (between 12-24 hours).

- Inspect the jars for broken seals, then wash the jars and dry them thoroughly before labeling them appropriately.

- Ensure the jams are stored in a cool, dry place where direct sunlight cannot reach.

11. Unsealed Jars

- If you discover your jars are unsealed, there are three options for you.

  - Firstly, take off the lid and band, check for a chipped rim, the presence of food residuals on the rim, and damage to the lid. You can replace the jars if necessary or reprocess the jar following the steps discussed above not later than a day.

  - Secondly, store the jar in the refrigerator and use it up not later than three days.

  - Lastly, you can adjust the headspace to one and a half inches and freeze (not refrigerate).

However, use up the product between six-nine months.

Adjusting Altitude For Home Canning

Before starting the pressure canning process, it is vital to know the altitude of where you live. For instance, South Dakota's altitude range is between 1,200-6,000 ft. above sea level. A person living in an area of 1,200 ft. would have to increase the processing time by 5 minutes in a boiling water bath canner, for instance. The increased processing time ensures the killing of pathogenic agents, thereby keeping the canned food safe. Instead of increasing the processing time when pressure canning, the pounds of pressure are increased. The table below gives the required time adjustments following the altitude.

The processing time should not be decreased in any pressure canners. To find the altitude of your locality, go to your local planning commission, zonal office, or a website about your city. Alternatively, you can download the Altimeter App to find the altitude of your locality or by checking the website, www.whatismyelevation.com.

BOILING WATER BATH CANNERS

Feet Above Sea Level	Increase in Processing Time
1,001-3,000	5 minutes
3,001-6,000	10 minutes
6,001-8,000	15 minutes
8,001-10,000	20 minutes

PRESSURE CANNERS

Feet Above Sea Level	Weighted-Gauge (Pounds of Pressure)	Dial-Gauge (Pounds of Pressure)
0-1,000	10	11
1,001-2,000	15	11
2,001-3,000	15	12
3,001-6,000	15	13
6,001-8,000	15	14
8,001-10,000	15	15

Chapter 4

Canning Mistakes and How to Avoid Them

Using a Boiling Water Bath Instead of a Pressure Canner

If you are to can foods with high acid levels like fruits, sweet preserves, pickles, and tomatoes (acidified), you need a boiling water bath, not a pressure canner. However, if you are to can foods with low acid levels like meat, soup stocks, and unpickled vegetables, you should use a pressure canner, which is different from a pressure cooker. Hot water bath canning is mainly for foods with high acidic levels.

Forgetting to Adjust The Canning Time or Pressure for Your Altitude

Depending on your location, you must adjust your canning time to the required altitude. The table in chapter three gives the required time adjustment for your water bath canning and the pressure adjustment for pressure canning. See chapter three for more information.

Overfilling The Jars

When canning, recipes usually indicate the headspace required to be left (½-1 inch). Ensure you comply with this directive as stated in your recipe. If you overfill the jars, it will result in a broken seal, which requires you to consume the food immediately or refrigerate and use it up within three days, depending on the food product.

Reusing Canning Lids

Except you are using tattler reusable lids, do not reuse your canning lids as this can lead to jars with broken seals.

Using Cracked or Chipped Canning Jars

Check your jars to ensure no cracks or chips on the rims, as they can lead to broken jars or seals.

Using Insufficient Water in a Boiling Water Bath

Before processing your jars, ensure they are submerged in water (1-2 inches). This makes the heating of the food even across every side.

Not Allowing The Jars Cool Before Moving Them

Always allow the jars to cool off completely before you move them; do not attempt to cool them using different means. Let them cool off naturally. Moving them too quickly can result in broken seals.

Using Low-Quality Ingredients

The quality of the products you use for your canning determines the quality of your canned food. Poor quality products can lead to spoilage of your stored food products.

Taking Jars Out of The Canner Too Soon

Resist the urge to take out the jars too soon; do not allow the excitement of carrying out your first canning successfully to tempt you into taking them out from the canners before the required time. Allow the jars to remain in the canners for at least five minutes after the heat is off, which helps prevent or minimize the risk of siphoning. After waiting, you can remove the jars and place them on a kitchen towel.

Forgetting To Wipe The Rims of The Jar

Another common mistake when canning is not wiping the rims of the jar after filling them up. Take time to carefully wipe off leftovers and spills on the side of the jars using a wet kitchen towel or a wet paper towel before processing. Not wiping the rims clean can result in improper sealing or broken seals. Ensuring that wiping the rims is part of your canning procedures would ensure this step is not skipped easily.

Leaving The Air Bubbles In The Jar

There is a reason for all procedures discussed in every canning process, do not neglect or skip any of the steps, as this can waste your time, food products, and money. Use a kitchen knife or bubble remover to let out the air bubbles in your jars. Air bubbles can spoil the food, increase the headspace in the jars, and aid the growth of bacteria.

Storing The Jars With The Rings/Bands On

The final of the twelve commonly made canning mistakes is the storage of the jars with the rings on. After the cooling time between (12-24 hours), ensure you label the jars accordingly and store them at a cool temperature and a place where direct sunlight cannot reach. If you do not remove the rings before storage, this can lead to different problems.

It is important to note that even with the rings on, the jar lids can become loose, leaving the jar unsealed, and air can penetrate the jars, adding bacteria growth.

If you store the jars without removing the rings, it might be difficult to detect an unsealed jar, only to spot it when you want to consume it, which will probably have affected the quality of the stored food, and bacteria could have grown in the canned food. Do not eat a stored with a bad seal to avoid botulism and food poisoning.

Furthermore, the rings can accommodate rust and mold; they retain some trapped moisture which may result in the ring being stuck on the jars. Ensure to remove the rings from the jars before storage.

A Short message from the Author:

Hey, I hope you are enjoying the book? I would love to hear your thoughts!

Many readers do not know how hard reviews are to come by and how much they help an author.

I would be incredibly grateful if you could take just 60 seconds to write a short review on Amazon, even if it is a few sentences!

>> Click here to leave a quick review

Thanks for the time taken to share your thoughts!

Chapter 5

Water Bath Canning FAQs

Do I have To Sterilize My Canning Jar?

No matter how glossy your new mason jar looks at first sight or how clean you feel your shelf is, always remember that in your shelves and hands are bacteria and spores that can only be seen with the use of a microscope. Therefore, sterilizing your mason jar will eliminate the risks of storing food along with these bacteria and spores, which you cannot see with ordinary eyes and simultaneously help your food stay fresh and perfectly healthy for a long period of time.

In your quest to discover the best way of flawlessly sterilizing your new mason jar, there are several options you can choose from, and they include; putting the jar in a dishwasher, in an oven, or on a stovetop for a specific amount of time. However, these methods are not scientifically accurate and are therefore not advisable. The best of these methods, which is scientifically proven, is to completely immerse your supposedly "clean jar" in 100°c boiling water.

How Can I Sterilize My Canning Jar?

The process of sterilizing canning jars is not rocket science but a simple and complete immersion of these jars in boiling water. Outlined below are step-by-step methods of sterilizing your mason jars. And this process should span for a period of twenty-five minutes.

1. First and foremost, wash cans in hot water, making sure to completely rinse any form of detergent on them, and place jars with their right side up in the water bath canner.

2. Fill all jars and water bath canner with hot water (note; hot water and not boiling water).

3. The next step is to raise the temperature of water to a hundred degrees celsius by using high heat.

4. Once the water gets to its boiling point, set your timer and boil mason jars. The amount of time you have to use to boil the jars depends solely on your sea level altitude.

5. When the timer gives off a beep, turn off the heat supply to the water bath, and pick up your

sterilized mason jar using a jar picker, then place them on a clean surface. Your sterilized canning Jar is now ready to use.

Why Do Canning Jars Break In a Water Bath?

Many people shy away from sterilizing mason jars due to fear of breakage. The process is just simple physics known as a thermal shock that comes into play. In order to prevent the jars from breaking, below are guidelines that you can follow:

- Make sure you put hot water into the canning jar before placing it into the water bath of boiling water. Also, ensure that the water in the canning jar is not hotter or way cooler than that of the water bath because this will make the glass jar expand quickly to a breaking point so as to cope with the sudden change in temperature and pressure.

- Watch out for cracks or weak points when shopping for your canning jars to avoid the risk of breakage when sterilizing the jars or storing foods in them. Also, avoid using commercial jars of poor quality like mayonnaise jars or recycled jars, no matter how economical they might seem.

What Happens If a Jar Breaks During Canning?

When a mason jar breaks, it does so subtly. You get to know when the timer gives off a beep or when you observe stored food staying afloat in the jar. When you notice this, do not panic but carefully separate this broken jar from the good jars, and clean out the broken jar and food properly. Do not attempt to make use of the food because it may contain fragments of broken glass.

Can You Boil Canning Jars Without A Rack?

It is not uncommon to get a water bath canner from either a nearby store, an online store, or a thrift store without the rack. When you are not lucky enough to get one with a rack, do not carelessly place your mason jar directly on the base of your canner, as this will increase the chances of your mason jars getting broken. Instead, try to improvise by searching for an accurate replacement for a rack so that the heat can uniformly circulate around the jars and minimize direct contact with the heat source.

Since the purpose of using a rack is to keep the jar from having direct contact with the canner, it is quite easy to be creative about finding and using alternatives when a rack is not readily available. You can order a new rack, or improvise by finding a perforated circular lightweight metal that can fit correctly into the canner and withstand heat.

Another creative way of improvising is to construct one using simple aluminum foil. To accomplish this, tear off seven pieces of aluminum foil, making sure that they are not more or less than two inches wide. After doing that, roll up these individual foils into a rope, then take three of these ropes and crimp each end to the other to form a firm circle. When the circle is in place, take the remaining four lengths of foil and weave them within and outside the circle in a zigzag manner, making sure to firmly clamp the ends.

When Should I Start Timing Hot Water Bath?

After filling the canner to the brim, ensure that the heat supply to the canner is at its highest and leave the water to boil with the lid firmly on the canner. When the water reaches its boiling point of hundred degrees celsius, you can then set your timer. To achieve a perfect canning result, ensure you get information on the accurate time your canning recipe needs.

How Long Does It Take For Canning Jars To Seal?

The canning process eliminates air present in the jar and food substances, but this doesn't occur in all cases. In the course of canning, the formation of a vacuum spurs the jar lid to seal up towards its rim. A unique way to detect that your canning jar has successfully sealed up is when it gives off a ping or pop sound and this occurs most of the time after the jars have completely cooled down. The amount of time it takes for a jar to seal largely depends on the item you are canning and it might take up to an hour or even more for your mason jar to completely seal.

How Do You Test Home Canned Jars For Proper Seal?

In cases whereby canned jars did not give off that peculiar notification of a ping sound, outlined below are a few ways of testing for a tight seal.

1. With your dominant hands, push down the center of the lid and observe closely what happens next. If the jar is well sealed, the lid will

remain flat on the jar. If the lid pops out, then the jar has not been sealed successfully.

2. There are certain sealants that come with canning lids, and their unique function is to seal up the rim of your mason jars. Once you detect that this unique function of the sealant has been achieved, remove the metal ring with caution and use your fingers to inspect the seal. The seal should be firmly attached to the rim, otherwise, the jar is not properly sealed.

What Do I Do If a Jar Doesn't Seal After Canning?

When your canning jar does not seal successfully, there should be neither a cause for regret or unnecessary alarm. There are many options to ensure your unsealed mason jar or its content does not end up as waste or in a trash can.

1. You can simply prepare the food as the day's meal to avoid wastage. You can also store a canning jar along with its content in a refrigerator and use it whenever it's convenient for you. The

microbial action of food substances is greatly reduced at extreme temperatures.

2. Your unsealed jar can also be reprocessed by firstly assessing the rim of your jar for a possible crack to ascertain the reason for the unsuccessful sealing. After confirming the possible reason, replace the mason jar with a new one, making sure to also use a new canning lid. Also, endeavor to follow accurately every instruction pertaining to the canning recipe peculiar to the food item you want to store.

Chapter 6

Recipes For Pickled Vegetables

Asparagus

Ingredients

For six (6) wide-mouth pint jars

- Ten (10) pounds of asparagus

- Six (6) big garlic cloves.

- Four (4) and a half (½) cups of water

- Four and a half (4½) cups of white distilled vinegar (5%)
- Six (6) little hot peppers (though optional)
- Half (½) cup of canning salt
- Three (3) tbs of dill seeds

For Seven (7) 12-ounce jars

- Seven (7) pounds of asparagus
- Seven (7) large garlic cloves
- Three (3) cups of water
- Three (3) cups of white distilled vinegar (5%)
- Seven (7) little hot peppers (though optional)
- One-third (⅓) cup of canning salt
- Two (2) teaspoons of dill seed

Instructions

1. Wash and rinse canning jars; sterilize accurately to destroy microorganisms and ensure the jar is kept hot until it's time for use. Read

manufacturer's instructions and prepare can lids accordingly.

2. Thoroughly rinse asparagus gently under clean flowing water. Remove stems from under the asparagus to make room for spears with tips that fit into the mason jar with a headspace of about half an inch. Skin and rinse garlic cloves thoroughly, then put a single garlic clove at the base of each mason jar and place firmly asparagus spears into your canning jars with the sharp ends up.

3. Mix water, salt, peppers (optional), vinegar, salt and dill seed in an 8-quart cauldron or dutch oven, and boil them. Then put one small pepper in each jar over the asparagus spears. Pour boiling pickling brine over prepared asparagus spears, leaving half an inch of headspace.

4. Make alterations to headspace if necessary and eliminate any possible air bubbles. Wipe the rim of the canning jars dry, and place a two-piece metal lid on the rim.

5. Process in a boiling water canner based on the altitudes adjustment table in chapter three.

6. After processing, pack raw, allowing the jars to cool down undisturbed for twelve to twenty-four hours, and finally, check the seals. Do not consume your stored pickled Asparagus immediately, but allow it to settle in the jars for about three to five days before use so as to retain and enhance its flavor.

Beets

Ingredients

- Seven (7) lbs of two (2) to two (2) and a half (½)-inch diameter of beets

- Four (4) cups of vinegar (5%)

- One-half (1 ½) teaspoons of canning or pickling salt
- Two (2) cups of sugar
- Two (2) cups of water
- Two (2) of cinnamon sticks
- Twelve (12) of whole cloves
- Four (4) to six (6) bulbs of onions (2-inch diameter)

Yield: Around 8 pints

Instructions

1. Peel off beet tops, leaving an inch of roots and stem to prevent its color from oozing out.

2. Rinse beet thoroughly and arrange in a pan of boiling water and cook for about twenty to twenty-five minutes until very tender.

3. After cooking, separate beets from liquid and leave to cool.

4. Cut off the roots, and stems and remove beet skin, then cut into one-fourth of inch slices.

5. Mix vinegar, sugar, salt and clean water together, then pour into a cheesecloth bag and add the required amount of spices. Pour sliced beets and onions into the cheesecloth bag and let it simmer for roughly five minutes.

6. Remove the bag and fill the jar with beets and onions, and hot vinegar mixture, leaving a headspace of about half an inch.

7. The next step is to process the canned beets in a boiling water canner based on the altitudes adjustment table in chapter three and pack using the hot pack method.

Dilled Beans

Ingredients

- Four (4) lbs of fresh tender green or yellow colored beans
- Eight (8) to sixteen (16) heads of fresh dill
- Eight (8) cloves of garlic
- Half (½) of canning salt
- Four (4) cups of white vinegar (5%)
- Four (4) cups of water
- One (1) tablespoon of hot red pepper flakes

Yield: Around 8 pints

Instructions

1. Take either your green or yellow beans and cut them into four inches in length.

2. Wash beans thoroughly, and trim the ends of beans.

3. In each sterile mason jar, arrange one to two dill heads and one clove of garlic, though this is optional.

4. Leaving a headspace of about half an inch, put whole dill beans upright, then add the boiled mixture of vinegar, salt, and water.

5. The final step is to process the dill beans according to the water bath canning altitudes in chapter three

Carrots

Ingredients

- Two-three quarter (2¾) pounds of peeled carrots (about three and a half (3½) pounds as purchased)

- Five and half (5½) cups of white distilled vinegar (5%)

- One (1) cup of water

- Two (2) cups of sugar

- Two (2) teaspoons of canning salt

- Eight (8) teaspoons of mustard seed

- Four (4) teaspoons of celery seed

Yield: Around 4 pints

Instructions

1. With precision, wash canning jars with detergent and rinse thoroughly; make sure the jar stays hot until it's ready for use. After studying the manufacturer's instructions, prepare the bands and lids accordingly.

2. Wash and skin the carrots well and cut carrots in circles that are approximately half an inch thick, or better still, cut them into strips.

3. Put two teaspoons of mustard seed and one tablespoon of celery seed in every clean hot mason jar. Then in a dutch oven, mix sugar, salt and vinegar together and boil with caution for about three minutes. Add carrots and bring to simmer until the carrots are partially cooked for about ten minutes.

4. Pour hot carrots into hot jars, making sure to leave a headspace of about one inch. Then cover hot carrot with hot pickling liquid and leave half an inch of headspace, making sure to remove bubbles.

6. Clean the rims of mason jars with a clean towel and place a two-piece metal canning lids. The final step is to process the canned carrots to the water bath canning altitudes in chapter three

5. After due processing, assess lids for proper sealing and allow them to sit for roughly three to five days before consumption.

Jerusalem Artichoke

Ingredients

- Two (2) gallons of Jerusalem artichokes

- Vinegar (5%)

- Two (2) cups of canning salt

- Four (4) tablespoons of turmeric

- Ten to twelve (10–12) medium-sized red peppers

Ingredients for Pickling Solution

- One (1) gallon of vinegar (5%)

- Thirteen (13) cups of sugar

- Half (½) cup of pickling spice (strapped in a spice bag)

73

- Two (2) tablespoons of turmeric

Yield: Around 10 or 12 pints

Instructions

1. Scrub Jerusalem artichokes thoroughly and cut them into generous sizes. Take these chunks, arrange them in a plastic container, and cover them with the required amount of vinegar. Add two cups of canning salt and turmeric, then mix thoroughly. After properly incorporating the mixture, set aside for twenty-four hours.

2. Thirty minutes before the twenty-four hours elapses, begin to sort the pickling solution by mixing a gallon of vinegar, pickling spice, sugar, and turmeric in a large pot. Then allow to simmer for about twenty to twenty-five minutes

3. Drain Jerusalem artichokes, and discard the liquid. Load Jerusalem artichokes into hot mason jars, packing raw, then add a medium-sized red

pepper to each jar, making sure to leave half an inch of headspace.

4. Pour in hot pickling solution into the jar, making sure to remove bubbles and properly adjusting the headspace to roughly half an inch. Clean the rims of jars with a paper towel, and fix in your metal canning lids.

5. Finally, process the canned Artichoke in a boiling water canner according to the altitudes in chapter three

Marinated Whole Mushrooms

Ingredients

- Seven (7) lbs of small whole mushrooms

- Half (½) cup of lemon juice

- Two (2) cups of olive oil

- Two (2)cups of white vinegar (5%)

- One (1) tablespoon of oregano leaves

- One (1) tablespoon of dried basil leaves

- One (1) tablespoon of canning salt

- Half (½) cup of finely diced onions

- One-quarter (¼) cup of chopped pimento

- Two (2) garlic cloves, cut in quarters

- Twenty-five (25) black peppercorns

Yield: Around 9 pints

Instructions

1. Pick out virginal mushrooms with caps below one to one-quarter of an inch in diameter.

2. Wash the mushrooms properly and cut out stems making sure to leave one-quarter of an inch fixed to the cap.

3. Cover trimmed mushrooms with lemon juice and simmer for about five minutes. Incorporate olive oil, oregano, vinegar, basil, and the right quantity of salt in a clean dutch oven.

4. Add onions and pimento and supply direct heat till it reaches boiling point. Put one-quarter garlic clove and peppercorns in a half-pint jar. Fill jars with mushrooms and well-incorporated vinegar solution while still hot, leaving half an inch of headspace.

5. Make necessary adjustments to lids and process per the altitude of your location as covered in chapter three

Dilled Okra

Ingredients

- Seven (7) lbs of small okra pods

- Six (6) small hot peppers

- Four (4) tablespoons of dill seed

- Eight to nine (8–9) cloves of garlic

- 2/3 cup of canning salt

- Six (6) cups of water

- Six (6) cups of vinegar (5%)

Yield: Eight to nine (8-9) pints

Instructions

1. Thoroughly wash and cut the okra, then fill jars with okra making sure to leave a headspace of half an inch.

2. Mix peppers, salt, vinegar, dill seed, and water in a large pan and boil steadily, and put a clove of garlic in each jar.

3. Afterward, pour pickling solution over the okra while it is still hot, making sure to leave a headspace of half an inch.

4. Pack raw and process the pickled filled okra according to the water bath altitude adjustment table in chapter three.

Bell Peppers

Ingredients

- Seven (7) lbs firm bell peppers
- Three to one-half (3 ½) cups of sugar
- Three (3) cups of vinegar (5%)
- Three (3) cups of water
- Three (9) cloves of garlic
- Four to one-half (4 ½) tablespoons of canning salt

Yield: Nine (9) pints

Instructions

1. Wash the peppers thoroughly, cutting them into quarter sizes. Separate flesh from seed, cutting away any blemishes. Cut peppers into strips.

2. Boil a mixture of vinegar, sugar, and water for a minute, adding the peppers to the mixture and bringing it to a boil.

3. Put half a clove of garlic and a quarter teaspoon of salt in each properly sterilized half-pint

canning jar while doubling the quantity for pint jars. Pack hot and add finely cut pepper strips, covering with the hot vinegar solution with a headspace of about half an inch.

4. Adjust the lids and process in your canner per the altitude adjustment table in chapter three

Pearl Onions

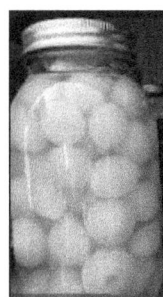

Ingredients

- Eight (8) cups of peeled white bulbs of pearl onions

- Five and a half (5 ½) cups of white distilled vinegar (5%)

- One (1) cup of water

- Two (2) teaspoons of canning salt

- Two (2) cups of sugar

- Eight (8) teaspoons of mustard seed

- Four (4) teaspoons of celery seed

Yield: Three to four (3-4) pint jars

Instructions

1. Prepare your mason jars by cleaning properly and preparing lids according to the manufacturer's instructions.

2. To peel onions, some should be placed on a strainer, then immerse gently in boiling water for thirty seconds. Remove onions and place in cold water for another thirty seconds. From the onion's root end and the other end, cut and peel about one-sixth of an inch slice.

3. In a clean stockpot, incorporate salt, sugar, vinegar and water thoroughly and boil steadily for three minutes. Add peeled onions to the

vinegar solution and simmer for about five minutes till the onions are partially cooked.

4. Two teaspoons of mustard seed and one teaspoon of celery seed should be placed into each clean, hot mason jar. Fill jars while they're still hot with the hot onions, leaving one-inch headspace. Leaving half an inch of headspace, cover onions with hot pickling solution and make sure to bubbles are removed.

5. Clean jar rims with a clean towel and process in a boiling water canner per the altitude adjustment table in chapter three

6. Remember to check for seals after twenty-four hours of letting it cool undisturbed, and let your pickled onions sit for about three to five days before consumption for flavor enhancement.

Spiced Green Tomatoes

Ingredients

- Six (6) pounds of small whole green tomatoes

- Nine (9) cups of sugar

- One (1) pint of cider vinegar (5%)

- Two (2) sticks of cinnamon

- One (1) tablespoon of whole cloves

- One (1) tablespoon of whole allspice

- One (1) tablespoon of whole mace or half (½) tablespoon of ground mace

Yield: About 4-pint jars

Instructions

1. Suitable alternatives for this pickle include green figs or plum tomatoes. Clean and peel tomatoes thoroughly. Create a solution of the vinegar, sugar, and spices. Put in all the tomatoes, boiling till they become clear.

2. Place tomatoes into hot jars making sure to leave half an inch headspace. Strain syrup and cover

tomatoes with the strained syrup while leaving a headspace of half-inch and eliminating air bubbles.

3. After cleaning the rims of the jar, process in a water bath canner per the altitude adjustment table in chapter three

Chapter 7

Recipes for Tomatoes, Sauces, and Salsas

Italian-Style Tomato Sauce

This recipe is the best for you if you're looking for a zero oil content tomato sauce with a classic Italian flavor. This recipe balances both naturally occurring and artificial acids for water bath canning. It is important not to go beyond the recommended ingredients and quantities to avoid processing a product that is unsafe for consumption due to abnormal changes in pH.

Ingredients

- Eight (8) cups of fresh tomato purée

- Two-thirds (2/3) cup of finely diced onion

- Two-thirds (2/3) cup of nearly chopped celery

- Half (½) cup of finely chopped carrot

- Two (2) cloves of finely chopped garlic

- Four (4) tablespoons of bottled lemon juice

- Two (2) tablespoons of canning salt

- Half (½) teaspoon of freshly ground black pepper

- Half (½) teaspoon of pepper flakes

- Mason jars with lids and bands

Yield: Three (3) pints

Instructions

1. Mix a cup of tomato puree, celery, carrots, onions, and garlic in a Dutch oven and boil the mixture carefully while stirring the contents.

2. Reduce the heat source, simmer vegetables for about five minutes, and add the remaining tomato puree one cup at a time.

3. Pour in lemon juice, black pepper, pepper flakes, and salt, then increase heat supply and boil thoroughly for about fifteen minutes while stirring until the mixture is reduced to about one-third.

4. Pour hot sauce into hot sterilized jars, remove air bubbles and leave half an inch of headspace.

5. Clean the canning jar's rim, fix the band, and adjust until it's tight.

6. Process filled mason jars in a boiling water canner for thirty-five (35) minutes, or per the altitude adjustment table in chapter three, and then allow the jar to sit undisturbed for twenty-four hours. Afterward, check the lid for a proper seal.

Herbed Tomato Juice

Using water bath canning to preserve herbed tomato juice helps it to stay fresh for a whole year. Add dill, parsley, or basil to fresh tomato juice. Then preserve it through water bath canning for summertime taste all year round.

Ingredients

- Twenty-five (25) lb of ripe medium-sized tomatoes

- Bottled lemon juice

- Fresh dill, basil, or parsley

- Twelve (12) glass canning jars with lids and bands

Instructions

1. Heat mason jars steadily in simmering water until time for use. Also, clean lids thoroughly in warm soapy water.

2. Wash tomatoes thoroughly and drain. Separate tomato flesh from its seed and ends, cut into generous quarters, pour quarters in a large

saucepan, and simmer under-regulated heat until soft, stirring to avoid sticking.

3. Using a food processor, juice the tomatoes, drain the juice, and set aside the seeds and tomato peels.

4. Place juice under-regulated heat (190ºF) for five(5) minutes.

5. Pour in half a teaspoon of citric acid or bottled lemon juice into each hot mason jar, then pour hot tomato juice into hot canning jars making sure to leave a headspace of a quarter inch.

6. Also, add fresh herbs to each jar, clean rims, then finally process filled jars in a boiling water canner for about thirty-five to forty minutes or based on the altitude adjustment table in chapter three.

7. Remove jars and set them aside for twenty-four hours, after which you check for seals.

Tomato Ketchup

This homemade canned ketchup is simply the best when compared to commercial brands. It has a more enriched flavor, well-regulated sugar, and salt and is undoubtedly healthier.

Ingredients

- Three (3) tablespoons of celery seeds

- Four (4) tablespoons of garlic cloves

- Two (2) sticks of cinnamon broken into pieces

- One and a half (1 ½) teaspoon whole allspice

- Three (3) cups of vinegar

- Twenty-four (24) lbs of medium-sized tomatoes, peeled with seeds and cores removed.

- Three (3) cups of chopped medium-sized onions

- One (1) tablespoon of cayenne pepper

- One and a half (1 ½) cups of granulated sugar

- One-quarter (¼) cup of canning salt

Yield: Seven pints

Instructions

1. Start by creating a spice bag by binding cloves, celery seeds, allspice, and cinnamon sticks tightly together.

2. Mix the newly created spice bag with vinegar in a clean saucepan, and bring to a boil. After boiling, set aside for twenty-five minutes, then discard the spice bag.

3. In another steel saucepan, incorporate cayenne, tomatoes, and onions, then boil over high heat, stirring as you go along. After boiling, reduce the heat source and let it simmer for about twenty minutes. Pour in your infused vinegar solution and boil with caution until the mixture thickens and you notice the vegetables soften. Using a food processor or a cheesecloth, extract liquid in batches, then dispose of solids afterward.

4. Bring drained liquid to the saucepan, then throw in some sugar and salt and boil gently or on medium heat, making sure to stir constantly until the consistency is like that of commercial ketchup. Do this for about forty-five minutes; the volume of the liquid will reduce by half and thicken considerably.

5. Pour hot ketchup into hot jars, ensuring you get rid of air bubbles as you poor, and accurately leave a headspace of half an inch.

6. Fix lids according to the manufacturer's instructions and process in a water bath canner for fifteen minutes, or adjust your altitude accordingly.

7. Check for proper seal after setting aside for twenty-four hours.

Basil-Garlic Tomato Sauce

This recipe is a nourishing combination of tomatoes, garlic, and basil for a sauce rich in flavor and free from microbial activity.

Ingredients

- Twenty (20) lb of medium-sized tomatoes (about 60 medium)

- One (1) cup of chopped onion

- Eight (8) cloves of garlic, finely diced.

- One (1) tablespoon of olive oil

- One-quarter (¼) cup of finely chopped, fresh basil

- Each hot jar has one-quarter (¼) tablespoon of citric acid or a tablespoon of bottled lemon juice

Yield: About seven (7) pints or three-quart glass canning jars

Instructions

1. Under controlled heat supply, place jars and lids in simmering water for heating until time for use. Also, prepare a boiling water canner, and set bands aside.

2. Wash tomatoes thoroughly and gently, then separate the flesh from cores and seeds. Chop into generous quarters and set aside

3. Pan-fry onion and garlic in olive oil till it gets translucent. Pour in tomatoes and bring to boil. Afterward, reduce heat supply and simmer for twenty minutes, stirring occasionally.

4. Separate tomato from its peel and seeds and blend till it becomes a smooth paste. Afterward, incorporate tomato puree and basil in a clean dutch oven and bring to boil. Reduce heat and simmer until the volume is reduced by half, making sure to stir as you go along to avoid sticking.

5. Pour the required amount of citric acid or lemon juice into each hot mason jar and fill it with steaming tomatoes, leaving about half an inch of headspace, which removes bubbles. Fix the lids

and adjust the band according to the manufacturer's instructions.

6. Process canning jars in a boiling water canner for about thirty-five to forty minutes or based on your location's altitude, as described in chapter 3.

7. Remove jars and let them sit undisturbed for twenty-four hours, then check for seal.

Harissa Sauce

This classical Moroccan-styled sauce is ideal for improving any dish's overall outlook and taste. Its rich red color alone speaks volumes.

Ingredients

- Four (4) red peppers, sauteed, peeled, and chopped.

- Eight (8) red chili, roasted, well seeded, and finely diced

- One (1) large onion, finely diced

- Six (6) cloves of garlic minced nicely

- Five (5) tablespoons of tomato paste

- Three-fourth (¾) cup of apple cider vinegar

- One (1) teaspoon of smoked paprika

- One (1) teaspoon of cumin seeds

- One (1) teaspoon of sugar

- Two (2) teaspoons of canning salt

Yield: Eight (8) oz half-pint jar

Instructions

1. Mix all the ingredients in a stainless steel saucepan and bring to a boil over medium heat.

Afterward, reduce heat, and simmer until the onions soften, then use a handheld food processor to make the harissa into a fine or chunky puree of desired consistency.

2. Prepare your canning tools accordingly and leave mason jars hot till ready for use.

3. Pour hot harissa sauce into a hot mason jar ensuring total elimination of air bubbles and leaving a headspace of half an inch.

4. Clean the rim of the jar and fix lids and bands accurately, then process in a boiling water canner for fifteen minutes or more based on your altitude as given in chapter 3.

5. Leave undisturbed after being fully processed for twenty-four hours, then check for seals.

Chili Sauce

This homemade chili sauce, made with traditional fresh Thai chilis and quality chill powder, beats factory-made standards. What makes it worth trying is the tinge of sweetness from brown sugar and the unique quality of this homemade sauce. This recipe goes well with hotdogs.

Ingredients

- Nine (9) lbs. of tomatoes, peeled and roughly chopped

- Six (6) bulbs of onions, finely chopped

- Three (3) red bell peppers, seeded and neatly chopped

- Six (6) Thai red or Anaheim chilis, seeded and neatly chopped

- Six (6) cloves of garlic

- Two (2) cups of apple cider vinegar

- One (1) cup of light brown sugar

- One (1) tablespoon of canning salt

- One (1) tablespoon of mustard seed

- One (1) tablespoon of grated horseradish (though optional)

- Two (2) tablespoons of chili powder

- Two (2) teaspoons of allspice

Yield: About eight (8) jars

Instructions

1. Put tomatoes, red peppers, onions, garlic, and chilies in a food processor, work in batches and blend into desired consistency.

2. Incorporate all ingredients in a clean dutch oven and boil over high heat, frequently stirring to avoid clumping. Afterward, reduce heat and simmer for about an hour until the sauce is thick enough to hold shape on the scoop. Remember to

stir occasionally while the sauce is simmering to avoid scorching.

3. Prepare your canning tools accordingly and leave mason jars hot till ready for use.

4. Pour hot chili sauce into hot mason jars, removing air bubbles and leaving a headspace of half an inch. Clean jar rims and fix lids and bands, making necessary adjustments before placing them in the boiling water canner.

5. Let sauce process for twenty minutes, making slight alterations for altitudes based on your location. After processing, set aside for twenty-four hours, then check for seals.

Chocolate Raspberry Sauce

This sauce is one to fall in love with on first taste effortlessly. Its use is limitless because the rich flavor combines with almost anything to produce a perfect taste that is healthy for consumption. Apart from serving desserts and fruits, it can be curated as a deeply appreciated gift.

Ingredients

- Half (½) cup of sieved unsweetened cocoa powder

- Six (6) tablespoons of classic Pectin

- Four and a half (4 ½) cups of mashed red raspberries

- Six three-quarters (6 ¾) cups of granulated sugar

- Four (4) tablespoons of bottled lemon juice

Yield: Six (6) half-pint jars

Instructions

1. Mix cocoa powder and pectin in a glass bowl, stirring until everything is evenly distributed. Set aside and mix mashed raspberries and lemon

juice in a clean steel saucepan. Pour in the pectin mixture and whisk until dissolved. Transfer mixture to a high heat source, and boil while stirring for about one minute. Afterward, turn off the heat, skimming off the foam.

2. Pour hot sauce into your hot mason jars, ensuring a headspace of a quarter inch. Fix in lids and adjust bands according to the manufacturer's instructions.

3. Finally, put jars in a boiling water canner and process for ten minutes while also considering your altitude for necessary adjustments.

4. After proper processing, remove jars, set them aside, and check lids for seals.

Peach Rum Sauce

This homemade recipe creates a rich, flavorful sauce that makes your deserts worth a glorious hype and far better than commercial brands. Its texture when warm is flavorsome, especially when eaten with ice cream.

Ingredients

- Six (6) cups of diced jagged and skinned peaches, treated to avoid browning and sieved

- Two (2) cups of delicately packed brown sugar

- Two (2) cups of granulated sugar

- Three-fourth (¾) cup of rum

- One (1) teaspoon grated lemon zest

- Seven (7) half-pint mason glass jars with their lids and bands

Yield: Seven (7) half-pint jars.

Instructions

1. Prepare your canning tools accordingly and leave mason jars hot till ready for use.

2. Incorporate all the ingredients in a large saucepan and boil over high heat, stirring until the brown sugar dissolves.

3. Reduce heat and boiling intensity, stirring when necessary for about twenty minutes until the mixture thickens to your desired consistency.

4. Pour hot sauce into your mason jars, eliminating air as you pour and leaving an accurate headspace of one-fourth inch.

5. Clean the rims and fix lids and bands according to the manufacturer's instructions.

6. Transfer hot jars to the boiling water canner and process for ten minutes while also considering your altitude for necessary adjustments.

7. After due processing, remove jars and set them aside for twenty-four hours, then check for seals.

Barbecue Sauce

Making a perfect grill starts with a perfect homemade barbecue sauce made with fresh and healthy ingredients. This recipe is just for you if you want to be popular in your neighborhood for making the tastiest grills.

Ingredients

- Twenty (20) cups of chopped seeded, peeled medium-sized tomatoes

- Two (2) cups of finely diced medium-sized onions (about 3 to 4 medium)

- Three (3) cloves of finely chopped garlic.

- One (1) tablespoon of hot pepper flakes

- One (1) Tablespoon of celery seeds

- One (1) cup of lightly packed brown sugar

- One (1) cup of white vinegar

- One-third (1/3) cup of lemon juice

- Two (2) tablespoons of salt

- One (1) tablespoon of finely ground mace or nutmeg

- One (1) tablespoon of dry mustard

- One (1) teaspoon of finely ground ginger

- One (1) teaspoon of finely ground cinnamon

Yield: About three (3) pint jars

Instructions

1. Mix tomatoes, garlic, hot pepper flakes, onions, and celery seeds in a large steel saucepan and boil over high heat, frequently stirring to avoid crimping. Lower heat source and boil steadily for about thirty minutes while covered till the vegetables soften.

2. Pour the mixture into a food mill or sieve to separate the liquid from the pulp. After proper extraction, discard the solids.

3. Return both liquid and pulp to the stainless steel saucepan. Put vinegar, ginger, brown sugar, salt, lemon juice, mustard, cinnamon, and mace, then boil over regulated heat gently, for about thirty to forty-five minutes, making sure to stir repeatedly till you notice the consistency thicken like that of a commercial barbeque sauce.

4. Prepare your canning tools accordingly and leave mason jars hot till ready for use. Afterward, pour your hot sauce into hot mason jars, leaving half an inch of headspace.

5. Remove all air bubbles and clean jar rims, then fix your lids and bands according to the manufacturer's instructions.

6. Afterward, transfer to boiling water canner and process for twenty minutes while also considering your altitude for necessary adjustments.

7. When duly processed, allow the jar to sit undisturbed for twelve to twenty-four hours, then check for seals.

Salsa Ranchera

Need that tinge of indigenous Mexican taste? This recipe, a blend of jalapenos, roasted tomatoes, and onions, creates a Picante salsa that takes you to Mexico, especially when eaten with grilled steak, the well-known tacos, or fish.

Ingredients

- Three (3) lb of plum tomatoes

- Four (4) jalapeño peppers

- Four (4) cloves of garlic

- One (1) medium-sized white onion, cut precisely into ½-inch rings

- Two (2) tablespoons of salt

- Half (½) cup of fresh, finely chopped cilantro

- One-third (1/3) cup of fresh lime juice

Yield: Four-pint jars

Instructions

1. Pre-heat your oven to a temperature of 425°. Ladle a large baking tray with aluminum foil, then arrange cores of tomatoes, garlic cloves, jalapenos, and onions in one layer.

2. Roast for twenty minutes, remove garlic and continue roasting until vegetables are very soft. Afterward, transfer baked jalapenos to a clean bowl, cover with plastic wrap, and let it sit undisturbed for fifteen minutes.

3. Remove tomato skins and chop coarsely with garlic and onions; put chopped vegetables and

diced jalapeno pepper in a medium-sized saucepan, add salt and bring to boil under over-regulated heat for two minutes, stirring constantly. Add lemon juice and cilantro, then remove heat.

4. After properly preparing your canning tools, pour in hot salsa mixture into the mason jars while they're still hot. Remove any air bubbles and leave a headspace of about half an inch. Fix your lids and bands accurately based on the manufacturer's instructions to ensure proper seals.

5. Transfer canning jars into a boiling water canner and process based on your altitude for twenty minutes while also considering your altitude for necessary adjustments.

6. After due processing, turn off the heat and let jars sit undisturbed for twenty-four hours, after which you check for seals. A properly sealed jar will not flex when the center is pressed down.

Tomatillo Salsa

This recipe is made from fresh and perfectly healthy chilies, tomatillos, and cilantro to create an original Mexican flavor that pairs perfectly with Mexican dishes such as burritos, tortilla chips, fajitas, and quesadillas.

Ingredients

- Five and a half (5 ½) cups of chopped cored husked tomatillos

- One (1) cup of chopped large-sized onion

- One (1) cup of chopped medium-sized green chilies (about 2 medium)

- Four (4) minced garlic cloves

- Four (4) tablespoons of finely minced cilantro

- Two (2) teaspoons of ground cumin

- Half (½) teaspoon of canning salt

- Half (½) teaspoon of red pepper flakes

- Half (½) cup of vinegar

- Four (4) tablespoons of lime juice

Yield: About four half-pints or two pints

Instructions

1. Make your boiling water canner ready and heat jars in hot water under low heat until ready for use. Wash lids properly in soapy water while still warm, and set jar bands aside.

2. Incorporate all ingredients in a large stainless steel saucepan and boil. Afterward, reduce the heat and let it simmer gently for ten minutes.

3. Pour hot salsa into hot jars, ensuring to remove air bubbles and leave a headspace of half an inch. Fix in lids and adjust bands according to the manufacturer's instructions.

4. Finally, place jars in a boiling water canner and process for fifteen minutes for half-pint jars and twenty minutes for full-pint jars. After due processing, turn off the heat and let jars sit undisturbed for twenty-four hours, after which you can check for seals.

Roasted Tomato Chipotle Salsa

This is another rich Mexican-inspired homemade sauce made with tomatillos and smoked tomatoes combined with hot chipotle peppers, giving you a perfect blend for making flavourful grills and tasty Mexican dishes. When processing peppers for this recipe, endeavor to use gloves to avoid getting burned.

Ingredients

- Twelve (12) dried and stemmed chipotle chili peppers

- Twelve (12) dried, stemmed cascabel chili peppers

- Two (2) lbs. of husked tomatillos

- Two (2) lbs. of Italian plum tomatoes

- Two (2) small onions

- One (1) garlic divided into cloves

- Half (½) cup of vinegar and half (½) cup of lime juice

- Two (2) teaspoons of sugar

- One (1) teaspoon of canning salt

Yield: About six-pint jars

Instructions

1. Toast chilies and chipotle in a big dry skillet over medium heat, then steam in batches for thirty seconds per side until they release their distinctive smell.

2. Transfer pliable toasted chilies and chipotle to a stainless steel bowl and add two cups of hot water. Pin chilies to the bottom of the bowl with a weight and soak for about fifteen minutes until it gets soft.

3. Transfer chilies and liquid to a food processor and blend until it forms a smooth puree, then set aside.

4. Roast tomatoes, tomatillos, garlic, and onions beneath a broiler for fifteen minutes, and constantly turning to ensure all sides are properly roasted, till garlic and onions are sparingly blackened, and the tomatoes alongside tomatillos look blistered, blackened, and obviously soft.

5. Put the tomatillos and tomatoes in paper bags, seal the opening and let it sit undisturbed for fifteen minutes until it's cool enough to be chopped alongside garlic and onions. After dicing vegetables, set aside.

6. Pour roasted tomatoes and tomatillos in a food processor or blender and blend until it forms a smooth puree, then set aside.

7. Make ready your boiling water canner and heat jars in hot water under low heat until ready for use. Wash lids properly in soapy water while still warm, and set jar bands aside.

8. Incorporate smooth tomatillo puree, roasted garlic and onions (already chopped), lime juice, vinegar, salt, and sugar in a large dutch pot. Boil combination on medium to high heat, making sure to stir frequently for about fifteen minutes until you are satisfied with the thickness.

9. Pour hot salsa into hot canning jars, leaving a headspace of half an inch and also ensuring total removal of air bubbles. If the need arises, add more sauce to attain the required headspace. Clean jar rims and fix the lid and bands according to the manufacturer's instructions.

10. Process salsa-filled canning jars in a boiling water canner based on altitude for fifteen minutes while also considering your altitude for necessary adjustments.

11. Remove jars after due processing, cool, and check for proper seal after twenty-four hours.

Corn and Cherry Tomato Salsa

This Salsa recipe is a delicious condiment made with a careful combination of fresh cherry tomatoes and corn kernels mixed with jalapenos and lime juice. This sauce can be taken any time of the year and fits with any dish of your choice.

Ingredients

- Five (5) lbs. of roughly diced cherry tomatoes

- Two (2) cups of fresh large-eared corn kernels

- One (1) cup of finely chopped red onion

- Two (2) teaspoons of canning salt

- Half (½) cup of branded lime juice

- Two (2) jalapeno peppers with their seeds removed and finely chopped

- One (1) teaspoon of chipotle chili powder

- Half (½) cup of fresh cilantro, finely chopped

- Six(6) glass mason jars with lids and bands

Yield: About six-pint jars

Instructions

1. Make your boiling water canner ready and heat jars in hot water under low heat until ready for use. Wash lids properly in soapy water while still warm, and set jar bands aside.

2. Incorporate all ingredients in a large stainless steel saucepan, and boil. Afterward, stirring occasionally, reduce the heat and let it simmer for five to ten minutes.

3. Pour the hot salsa into a hot mason jar, eliminating any bubbles and maintaining a headspace of about half an inch. Fix the lid, adjust

bands according to the manufacturer's instructions, and transfer all the jars to the boiling water canner.

4. Process the salsa-laden jars for fifteen minutes while also considering your altitude for necessary adjustments.

5. After properly processing salsa, remove and let it stand for five minutes. Take your time to check for seals after twenty-four hours.

Zesty Salsa

Nothing beats an indigenous salsa recipe with a tinge of a savory combination of preferred chill peppers and even daring hot pepper sauce, depending on how adventurous your taste buds are.

Ingredients

- Ten (10) cups of finely chopped, cored and peeled medium-sized tomatoes

- Five (5) cups of finely chopped seeded large green bell peppers

- Five (5) cups of finely diced medium-sized onions

- Two (2) cups of neatly chopped and seeded medium-sized chili peppers, such as jalapenos, Hungarian wax, and hot banana.

- One (1) cup of apple cider vinegar

- Three (3) cloves of finely diced garlic

- Two (2) tablespoons of finely chopped cilantro

- One (1) tablespoon of canning salt

- One (1) teaspoon of hot pepper sauce, though optional

Yield: About 6-pint jars (16 oz) or 12 half-pint jars (8 oz)

Instructions

1. Prepare your boiling water canner and heat jars in hot water under low heat until ready for use. Wash lids properly in soapy water while still warm, and set jar bands aside.

2. Mix fresh finely chopped tomatoes, onions, green pepper, chili peppers, garlic, vinegar, cilantro, hot pepper sauce, and the required amount of salt in a clean stainless steel saucepan. Boil mixture over medium to high heat and later reduce heat and simmer while stirring continuously for about ten minutes. Turn off the heat source once you're satisfied with the consistency.

3. Fill hot salsa into hot canning jars, ensuring a headspace of half an inch. Also, endeavor to remove air bubbles and fix the lids and bands according to the manufacturer's instructions.

6. Once that is done, transfer mason jars to a boiling water canner and process for fifteen minutes while also considering your altitude for necessary adjustments.

4. After proper processing, remove salsa-laced mason jars and set them aside for twenty-four hours, then check for seals.

Green Tomato Salsa Verde

Green tomatoes are very easy to find. You can use this to your advantage by making a rejuvenating salsa of fresh, healthy green tomatoes, jalapenos, cilantro, and lime juice. This recipe perfectly matches some tasty grilled fish tacos or crispy tortilla chips.

Ingredients

- Seven (7) cups of finely diced, cored, and peeled fresh medium-sized green tomatoes.

- Five to ten (5-10) habanero peppers or jalapenos with their seed removed and finely diced.

- Two (2) cups of finely chopped large red onions (about 2 large)

- Two (2) cloves of finely chopped garlic

- Half (½) cup of lime juice

- Half (½) cup of loosely packed and chopped cilantro

- Two (2) teaspoons of ground cumin spice

- One (1) teaspoon of dried oregano leaves

- One (1) teaspoon of canning salt

- One (1) teaspoon of freshly ground black pepper

Yield: About six (6) half pints

Instructions

1. Prepare your boiling water canner and heat jars in hot water under low heat until ready for use. Wash lids properly in soapy water while still warm, and set jar bands aside.

2. Mix finely chopped tomatoes, onion, garlic, habanero peppers, and lime juice in a large clean stainless steel saucepan and boil. Pour in cumin spice, oregano leaves, salt, and black pepper, then reduce heat supply, and simmer for five minutes.

3. Next up is to fill your prepared hot mason jars with hot salsa, removing air bubbles and maintaining a headspace of half an inch. Fix lids and bands according to the manufacturer's instructions to avoid wrong sealing.

4. Transfer mason jars containing salsa to the boiling water canner, and allow for processing while adjusting to altitude for about twenty minutes; also consider your altitude for necessary adjustments.

5. After processing, check lids for seals. A properly sealed mason jar will remain compressed when pressed down.

Chapter 8

Recipes for Jams, Jellies, and Marmalades

Apricot Jam

This recipe is a fine blend of beautiful fresh and sweet apricot fruits. Its slightly acidic nature contributes to its tingling sour taste, helping to preserve this homemade canned jam for long-term use.

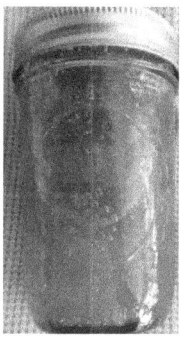

Ingredients

- Five (5) cups of peeled and jagged apricot halves

- Four (4) cups of sugar

- One-fourth (¼) cup of lemon juice

Yield: About four (4) half-pint mason jars

Instructions

1. Wash the whole apricots thoroughly with clean running water, then drain. Blanch in boiling water for about thirty to sixty seconds to peel the apricot.

2. After blanching, transfer to cold water immediately and remove the peel. Separate its flesh from pits, and measure out five apricot halves.

3. Mix prepared apricots, bottled lemon juice and granulated sugar in a large dutch pot. Afterward, cover and let it sit in the refrigerator for about four to five hours. Later on, boil the mixture and continue stirring until you can no longer observe traces of sugar. Remove from the heat source, skimming off foam if needed.

4. Pour hot apricot mixture into a hot mason jar, leaving a headspace of one-quarter of an inch and eliminating any possible air bubbles.

5. Clean the rims of the mason jar and transfer all jars to the boiling water canner for processing.

6. Process apricot-filled jars for fifteen minutes while also considering your altitude for necessary adjustments, and set them aside for twelve hours to ensure proper sealing.

Caramel Apple Coffee Jam

The caramel apple coffee jam is as delicious as it sounds. This easy-to-make recipe perfectly blends the unique taste of caramel with quality black coffee. Combining this jam with hot cinnamon rolls, fresh toast, or delectable ice cream gives your taste buds an unforgettable and mouthwatering experience. You can also incorporate this luscious jam into your scone batter before tossing it into the oven.

Ingredients

- Five (5) cups of peeled and nicely diced apples

- Two (2) cups of extra strong brewed coffee

- Four (4) tablespoons of ball pectin

- Half (½) teaspoon of ground allspice

- Two (2) cups of brown sugar

Yield: About four (4) half-pint jars

Directions

1. Under low to medium heat, place washed jars and lids in simmering water for heating until time for use. Also, prepare a boiling water canner, and set bands aside.

2. Place diced apples and brewed coffee in a clean stainless saucepan and let it boil. After boiling, reduce the heat source and allow it to simmer gently for about ten minutes. When you observe the apples to be very soft, pour them into a food processor and puree smoothly, then return to heat supply.

3. Add allspice and pectin and whisk thoroughly. Bring the whole mixture to a full boil that cannot be stirred. Pour in sugar, stirring well to dissolve, then boil on high heat rapidly for one minute. After it has come to a rolling boil, remove from heat and gently skim off foam.

4. Fill hot mason jars with hot jam ensuring a headspace of a quarter inch while removing air bubbles. Fix lids on jars and apply bands, ensuring to follow the manufacturer's instructions correctly.

5. Transfer all the filled jars into a boiling water canner and process for ten minutes while also considering your altitude for necessary adjustments.

6. After processing, let jars stand for twelve to twenty-four hours, after which you check for seals.

Strawberry Jam

Strawberries are summer's firstborn fruits rich in antioxidants and vitamins, especially vitamin C. The creative transformation of this fruit into an ageless tasty jam goes with yogurt, peanut butter, oven-ready biscuits, and grilled cheese.

Ingredients

- Five (5) cups of mashed strawberries
- One-quarter (¼) cup of lemon juice
- Six (6) tablespoons of Pectin
- Seven (7) cups of granulated sugar

Yield: Eight (8) half-pints

Instructions

1. Under low to medium heat, place washed jars and lids in simmering water for heating until time for use. Also, prepare a boiling water canner, and set bands aside.

2. Mix bottled lemon juice and strawberries into a clean dutch oven. Pour in pectin and stir gradually, then bring to a full boil, then stir constantly. Add the sugar and stir until there are no traces of sugar. Boil vigorously for a full minute, then remove from the heat source.

3. Fill hot canning jars with newly made jam, leaving a headspace of a quarter inch while removing air bubbles. Fix the lid on jars and apply bands following the manufacturer's instructions thoroughly.

4. Transfer filled jars to the boiling water canner and process for ten minutes while also considering your altitude for necessary adjustments.

5. After due processing, remove it from the heat source, and let it sit for twenty-four hours, after which you check for seals by compressing the center of the lid. A properly sealed jar lid will not flex after being compressed in the middle.

Strawberry Jam Variations

1. Vanilla Strawberry Jam

Get a vanilla bean, split it in half with precision, and then mix it with mashed strawberries. Cook as instructed above, and ensure to remove vanilla bean before transferring jam to the canning jars. The result is a strawberry jam with a unique vanilla flavor.

2. Strawberry Balsamic Jam

This recipe accentuates the flavor of the strawberry. You can achieve this by reducing the initial amount of lemon juice to just one tablespoon and adding three tablespoons of high-quality balsamic vinegar.

3. Lemony Strawberry Jam

Another brilliant twist to making a flavourful strawberry jam is to add finely grated lemon zest to the mashed strawberries.

4. Black Pepper Strawberry Jam

Give your taste buds a spicy experience by adding fresh, finely ground black pepper for a fresh-quality flavor into cooked strawberry jam before pouring it into canning jars.

Fig Jam

This rich flavored fig jam made with quality pectin perfectly combines well-made smoked meat and cheese.

Ingredients

- Four (4) cups of chopped medium-sized figs

- Half (½) cup of bottled lemon juice

- Half (½) cup of water

- One (1) 3-oz Liquid Fruit Pectin

- Half (½) teaspoon of butter or margarine

- Six (6) cups of sugar

Yield: Eight (8) half-pint jars

Instructions

1. Under low to medium heat, place washed jars and lids in simmering water for heating until time for use. Also, prepare a boiling water canner, and set bands aside.

2. Incorporate chopped figs with sugar, lemon juice, and water in a stainless steel saucepan, and add butter to limit the foaming. Bring mixture to boil over very high heat. After fully boiling, add pectin and stir while boiling hard for a full minute.

3. Pour hot fig jam into prepared mason jars, ensuring a headspace of a quarter inch and eliminating any bubbles. Fix lids and bands

accurately and transfer jars to the boiling water canner for processing per the water bath canning altitude adjustments table in chapter three.

4. After processing, remove from the heat source, set aside undisturbed for twenty-four hours, and then check for seals.

Black Raspberry Jam

Do you want to enjoy fresh and delicious tasting black raspberries for a full year? Then, you can achieve this by thoroughly following this recipe for a fulfilling jam adventure.

Ingredients

- Three (3) cups of crushed black raspberries

- One-quarter (¼) cup of bottled lemon juice

- One (1) 3-oz pouch of liquid Pectin

- Half (½) teaspoon of butter or margarine

- Seven (7) cups of sugar

Yield: Eight (8) half-pint jars

Instructions

1. Under low to medium heat, place washed jars and lids in simmering water for heating until time for use. Also, prepare a boiling water canner, and set bands aside.

2. Mix crushed raspberries with sugar and lemon juice in a stainless steel saucepan. Add butter to reduce the foam. Bring the mixture to a rolling boil over very high heat, ensuring to stir constantly.

3. Pour hot jam into hot mason jars, ensuring to remove air bubbles and leaving a headspace of a quarter inch. Fix lids and bands according to the manufacturer's instructions and transfer all the jars to the boiling water canner for processing per

the water bath canning altitude adjustments table in chapter three.

4. After proper processing, remove from heat and allow the jars to sit undisturbed for twenty-four hours, then check for seals. A properly sealed jar will have a lid that will not flex after being compressed.

Orange Jelly

This delicious jam made with unique fresh, tasting vitamin-rich orange and low-sugar pectin is your best bet for a healthy all-year-round feeding experience.

Ingredients

- Four (4) cups of freshly prepared orange juice

- Three (3) tablespoons of low sugar fruit Pectin

- Half (½) teaspoon of butter or margarine

- Three (3) cups of sugar

- One (1) cup of zero-calorie sweetener

- Three-fourth (3/4) to one (1) cup of honey

- Two (2) tablespoons of bottled lemon juice (optional)

Yield: Four to five half-pint jars

Instructions

1. Under low to medium heat, place washed jars and lids in simmering water for heating until time for use. Also, prepare a boiling water canner, and set bands aside.

2. Incorporate fresh orange juice and low-sugar pectin, ensuring to stir gradually. Add butter if needed to reduce foaming. Boil mixture over high heat if they cannot be stirred while also stirring frequently.

3. Add sweetener or honey per your required amount, and return to a high rolling boil. Boil vigorously for a full minute stirring frequently. Remove mixture from heat, skimming the foam.

4. Pour hot orange jelly into hot jars, leaving a headspace of one-quarter of an inch, ensuring to remove air bubbles.

5. Process orange-filled mason jars in a boiling water canner for about ten minutes based on your altitude.

6. After due processing, remove from the heat source and set aside for twenty-four hours, after which you can check for seals.

Pomegranate Jelly

Pomegranates are rich autumn fruits with daring flavor antioxidants, making them an excellent jelly for mouthwatering meals.

Ingredients

- Three (3) cups of prepared pomegranate juice

- Six (6) tablespoons of pectin

- Half (½) teaspoon of butter or margarine, though optional,

- Five (5) cups of sugar

Yield: Six half-pint jars

Instructions

1. Under low to medium heat, place washed jars and lids in simmering water for heating until time for use. Also, prepare a boiling water canner, and set bands aside.

2. Put fresh pomegranate juice in a clean saucepan and gradually stir in pectin. If you desire, add half a teaspoon of butter to reduce foaming. Bring the whole mixture to boil over very high heat, stirring vigorously.

3. Pour in sugar, stirring vigorously till all traces of sugar dissolve. Boil once again over high heat, ensuring constant stirring. Remove from heat after full boiling and fill hot jars with hot pomegranate jam ensuring a headspace of a quarter inch and removing air bubbles.

4. Transfer canning jars to the boiling water canner for processing. Process jars for about ten minutes while also considering your altitude for necessary adjustments.

5. Check for proper seals after twenty-four hours.

Tip: To prepare fresh pomegranate juice, roll the fruit on a countertop or flat surface to soften without damaging the skin. Hold the pomegranate over a fine sieve placed in a clean bowl, and use a sharp knife to cut out the crown and juice of the pomegranate. The juice will start to gush out as soon as you make an incision on the skin. Squeeze the pomegranate contents into the sieve and properly separate the juice from the pomegranate seeds after juicing, measuring about three and a half cups for your jam recipe.

Apple Jelly

*Without added pectin

Ingredients

- Four (4) cups of apple juice

- Two (2) tablespoons of freshly made lemon juice(optional)

- Three (3) cups of sugar

Yield: Four to five (4-5) half-pint jars

Instructions

1. Under low to medium heat, place washed and sterilized jars and lids in simmering water for heating until time of use. Also, prepare a boiling water canner, and set bands aside.

2. To make fresh apple juice, pick out one-fourth (¼) unripe and three-fourths (¾) of ripe apples. Wash apples and cut them into small pieces.

3. Pour into a clean saucepan with water and boil over high heat. After boiling, let it simmer over low heat for twenty minutes till the apples look very soft. Allow to cool and process properly to extract the juice.

4. To make tasty jelly, measure out four cups of apple juice into a dutch oven. Pour in lemon juice and sugar and incorporate them properly. Bring the whole mixture to a full rolling boil above the boiling point of water.

5. Douse hot canning jars with hot jelly ensuring to leave a headspace one-quarter of an inch.

6. Transfer canning jars to the boiling water canner for processing for ten to twenty minutes based on altitude. Check for seals after twenty-four hours.

Cherry Jelly

*With liquid pectin

Ingredients

- Three (3) cups of cherry juice

- Seven (7) cups of sugar

- Two (2) pouches of liquid pectin

Yield: About eight (8) half-pint jars

Instructions

1. Under low to medium heat, place washed and sterilized jars and lids in simmering water for heating until time for use. Also, prepare a boiling water canner, and set bands aside.

2. To make fresh cherry juice, pick out fully ripe cherries, wash thoroughly, and remove stems without pithing. Mash cherries, add water, pour into a clean pot, and boil vigorously. Afterward, reduce the heat and let it simmer for ten minutes, then extract the juice.

3. To make cherry jelly, pour the required amount of juice into a kettle, then add sugar. Boil over very high heat, making sure to stir vigorously. Add pectin and boil actively for a full minute. Remove from heat and pour into sterilized mason

jars, ensuring a headspace of one-quarter of an inch.

4. Process thoroughly in a boiling water canner per the water bath canning altitude adjustments table in chapter three.

Grape Jelly

*With liquid pectin

Ingredients

- Four (4) cups of grape juice,

- Seven (7) cups of sugar

- Half (½) bottle of liquid pectin

Yield: About eight (8) or nine (9) half-pint jars

Instructions

1. Under low to medium heat, place washed and sterilized jars and lids in simmering water for heating until time for use. Also, prepare a boiling water canner, and set bands aside.

2. To prepare fresh grape juice, wash thoroughly and remove stems from ripe fresh grapes. Mash grapes and add water, cover, and boil on very high heat. After boiling, reduce heat and simmer the mixture for ten minutes, then extract the juice.

3. Make the jelly by pouring the required amount of grape juice into a kettle and stirring in sugar. Put the mixture on very high heat and bring it to a full boil while stirring constantly. Toss in pectin and boil vigorously for a minute, then remove from heat and skim off excess foam.

4. Fill the sterile mason jars with hot jelly, making sure to leave about one-quarter headspace, and wipe rims clean with a paper towel. Fix lids and bands according to the manufacturer's instructions and process in a boiling water canner for five to fifteen minutes while also considering your altitude for necessary adjustments.

Apple Marmalade

*Without added pectin

Ingredients

- Eight (8) cups of thinly sliced apples

- One (1) orange

- One and a half (1½) cups of water

- Five (5) cups of granulated sugar

- Two (2) tablespoons of bottled lemon juice

Yield: About 6 or 7 half-pint jars

Instructions

1. Under low to medium heat, place washed and sterilized jars and lids in simmering water for

heating until time for use. Also, prepare a boiling water canner, and set bands aside.

2. Prepare fruit by selecting tart apples. Wash, peel, cut, and core the apples properly. Also, do the same to the orange and slice the orange and apple very thin.

3. To make marmalade jam, pour fruit mix, sugar, lemon juice, and water into a clean saucepan and boil over very high heat to about 9F above boiling point, stirring frequently. When you are satisfied with the consistency of the mixture, remove from heat and fill sterile mason jars with hot marmalade, then fix lids and bands according to the manufacturer's instructions.

4. Transfer mason jars into a boiling water canner and process marmalade jam for five to fifteen minutes based on altitude.

Citrus Marmalade

*Without added pectin

Ingredients

- Three-quarter (¾) cup of grapefruit peel

- Three-quarter (¾) cup of orange peel

- One-third (1/3) cup of lemon peel

- 1 quart of cold water

- A pulp of grapefruit

- Pulp of 4 medium-sized oranges

- 2 cups of boiling water

- 3 cups of sugar

Yield: 3 or 4 half-pint jars

Instructions

1. Under low to medium heat, place washed and sterilized jars and lids in simmering water for heating until time for use. Also, prepare a boiling water canner, and set bands aside.

2. Prepare fruits by washing and peeling the fruits, then cut peels into thin strips and place them in a

clean saucepan. Add water and simmer gently over low heat for about thirty minutes until very tender. Drain simmered peels, remove seeds and membranes from fruit and cut them into minute pieces.

3. Make a marmalade by incorporating the peels and fruit in a clean saucepan and adding boiling water and granulated sugar. Stir while boiling over high heat until its temperature is above that of boiling water for about twenty minutes. After boiling, remove from heat and skim excess foam.

4. Pour the hot marmalade into hot mason jars, ensuring a headspace of one-quarter of an inch. Transfer canning jars to a boiling water canner, fix lids and bands according to the manufacturer's instructions, and process between five to fifteen minutes based on the altitude adjustments table in chapter 3.

Cranberry Marmalade

*With powdered pectin

Ingredients

- Two (2) pulps of oranges

- One (1) pulp of lemon

- Three (3) cups of water

- Four (4) cups of cranberries

- One (1) box of powdered pectin

- Seven (7) cups of sugar

Yield: 10 or 11 half-pint jars

Instructions

1. Under low to medium heat, place washed and sterilized jars and lids in simmering water for heating until time for use. Also, prepare a boiling water canner, and set bands aside.

2. Remove the skin of the orange and lemon and finely chop the rinds. Place in a clean saucepan with water and boil. After a while, simmer for

twenty minutes. Chop the fleshy part of orange and lemon and cook with the rind of cranberries.

3. Prepare marmalade by incorporating the right measure of fruit into a clean kettle. Add water and pectin, then stir properly. Add sugar and bring the whole mixture to a full rolling boil till bubbles cover the entire surface.

4. Fill jars with marmalade while still hot, and transfer to boiling water canner after fixing lids and bands until the jars.

5. Process per the altitude adjustment table in chapter three.

Orange Marmalade

Ingredients

- Four (4) cups of thinly sliced orange peel
- Four (4) cups of cut-up orange pulp
- One (1) cup of thinly sliced lemon
- Six (6) cups of water
- Six (6) cups of sugar

Yield: 8 half-pint jars

Instructions

1. Under low to medium heat, place washed and sterilized jars and lids in simmering water for heating until time for use. Also, prepare a boiling water canner, and set bands aside.

2. Rinse oranges and lemons, peel both fruits, and slice rinds thinly. Remove membranes and seeds from orange and lemon pulp and cut them into small sections. Measure the required amount of fruits and pour them into a dutch oven. Boil together with the peel, water, and sugar, ensuring to stir until marmalade is formed.

154

6. Fill hot jars with marmalade ensuring a headspace of one-quarter of an inch. Wipe rims and fix lids and bands according to the manufacturer's instructions. Afterward, transfer jars to the boiling water canner and process per the altitude adjustment table in chapter three.

Tomato Marmalade

Ingredients

- Three (3) quarts of ripe tomatoes

- Three (3) oranges

- Two (2) lemons

- Four (4) sticks of cinnamon

- Six (6) whole allspice

- One (1) tablespoon of whole cloves

- Six (6) cups of sugar

- One (1) teaspoon of canning salt

Yield: Nine half-pint jars

Procedure

1. Under low to medium heat, place washed and sterilized jars and lids in simmering water for heating until time for use. Also, prepare a boiling water canner, and set bands aside.

2. Peel tomatoes, oranges, and lemons, and cut them into minute pieces. Tie spices together in a cheesecloth bag. Place vegetables, fruits, sugar, and salt in a large stainless steel saucepan and boil for about fifty minutes, stirring frequently.

3. After boiling, pour marmalade into a hot jar and process in a boiling water canner according to the altitude adjustment table in chapter three.

The end... almost!

Hey! We've made it to the final chapter of this book, and I hope you've enjoyed it so far.

If you have not done so yet, I would be incredibly thankful if you could take just a minute to leave a quick review on Amazon

Reviews are not easy to come by, and as an independent author with a little marketing budget, I rely on you, my readers, to leave a short review on Amazon.

Even if it is just a sentence or two!

So if you really enjoyed this book, please...

>> Click here to leave a brief review on Amazon.

I truly appreciate your effort to leave your review, as it truly makes a huge difference.

Chapter 9

Recipes for Chutneys and Relishes

Dill Pickle Relish

Ingredients

- Fourteen (14) cups of chopped pickling cucumbers

- Two (2) cups of chopped red bell pepper

- Five and a half (5½) cups of apple cider vinegar

- Three (3) teaspoons of dill seed

- Six (6) cloves of minced garlic

- Five (5) tablespoons of pickling or canning salt

Yield: Seven (7) pint jars

Instructions

1. Under low to medium heat, place washed and sterilized jars and lids in simmering water for heating until time for use. Also, prepare a boiling water canner, and set bands aside.

2. Wash pepper and cucumbers well enough and slice them into thin pieces; then chop in a food processor to create smaller pieces. Measure the right amount of cucumber and pepper and set it aside.

3. In a clean saucepan, add vinegar, dill seed, garlic, salt, and vegetables. Bring mixture to boil, then simmer over low heat for ten minutes.

4. Pour relish into hot mason jars, ensuring a headspace of half an inch, and process in a boiling water canner between fifteen to twenty-five minutes, taking into consideration your altitude as described in chapter three.

Sweet Pepper Relish

Ingredients

- Five (5) cups of ground green bell peppers

- Five (5) cups of ground red bell peppers

- One and a half (1½) cups of ground onion

- Two and a half (2 ½) cups of distilled vinegar (5%)

- Two (2) cups of sugar

- Four (4) teaspoons of canning salt

- Four (4) teaspoons of mustard seed

Yield: Six (6) pint jars

Instructions

1. Under low to medium heat, place washed and sterilized jars and lids in simmering water for heating until time for use. Also, prepare a boiling water canner, and set bands aside.

2. Prepare peppers and onions properly, and cut them into large pieces. Grind both pepper and onions coarsely and combine the mixture with its juice in a large saucepan. Add the remaining ingredients and boil over high heat. Afterward, reduce heat and simmer for thirty minutes, stirring constantly.

3. Fill sterile jars with hot relish making sure to leave a headspace of half an inch, and remove any bubbles. Adjust lids and bands, then process in the boiling water canner for about 10-20 minutes according to your altitude, as described in chapter three.

4. After processing, set aside for twenty-four hours, then check for seals.

Piccalilli

Ingredients

- Six (6) cups of chopped green tomatoes
- One and a half (1 ½) cups of chopped red peppers
- One and a half (1 ½) cups of chopped green peppers
- Two-quarter (2 ¼) cups of chopped onions
- Seven and a half (7 ½) cups of chopped cabbage
- Half (½) cup of canning salt
- Three (3) tablespoons of whole mixed pickling spice
- Four and a half (4 ½) cups of vinegar (5%)
- Three (3) cups of brown sugar

Yield: Nine half-pints

Instructions

1. Under low to medium heat, place washed and sterilized jars and lids in simmering water for heating until time for use. Also, prepare a boiling water canner, and set bands aside.

2. Prepare vegetables and mix with a half cup of salt. Immerse in hot water and let it stand for twelve hours, then drain.

3. Merge spices in a spice bag and add vinegar and sugar, then boil in a clean saucepan.

4. Pour in vegetables and boil gently for thirty minutes till you are satisfied with the consistency.

5. Fill sterile mason jars with the hot mixture and fix lids and bands correctly.

5. Afterward, put jars in a boiling water canner for processing between five to ten minutes according to your altitude, as described in chapter three.

Pear Relish

Ingredients

- Two (2) gallons of pears
- Six (6) large onions
- Six (6) sweet green peppers
- Six (6) sweet red peppers
- One (1) bunch of celery
- Three (3) cups of sugar
- One (1) tablespoon of allspice
- One (1) tablespoon of canning salt
- Five (5) cups of vinegar (5%)

Yield: 10-pint jars

Instructions

1. Wash and peel pears, peppers, celery, and onions in cold water. Remove seeds where necessary.

2. Place pear and vegetables in a food chopper to process. Add the remaining ingredients into the chopped combination and keep it in the refrigerator overnight.

3. Bring the relish mixture to a boil, then simmer gently for five minutes.

4. Place relish into hot mason jars. While eliminating air bubbles, ensure to leave a headspace of half an inch. Transfer jars into a boiling water canner after properly fixing lids and bands for processing.

5. Process between twenty to thirty minutes according to your altitude, as described in chapter three.

Hot Pepper Relish

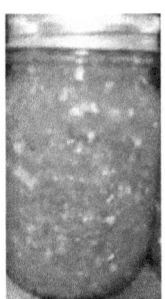

Ingredients

- Five (5) cups of ground green or red bell peppers

- Five (5) cups of ground jalapeno peppers

- One and a half (1½) cups of ground onion

- Two (2) cups of white vinegar (5%)

- Two (2) cups of sugar

- Four (4) teaspoons of canning salt

- Four (4) teaspoons of mustard seed

Yield: 6-pint jars

Instructions

1. Under low to medium heat, place washed and sterilized jars and lids in simmering water for

heating until time for use. Also, prepare a boiling water canner, and set bands aside.

2. Wash bell and jalapeno peppers well enough. Get rid of their stems and seeds and cut them into large pieces alongside clean onions. Grind both peppers and onions coarsely. Ensure you use gloves while cutting peppers to avoid getting burned.

3. Measure the right amount of peppers and jalapenos alongside their juices and incorporate these peppers with onions and the remaining ingredients in a large saucepan. Boil over high heat, then bring to a low boil for thirty minutes. Ensure to stir frequently to avoid scorching.

4. Pour freshly made relish into sterile mason jars, ensuring a headspace of half an inch. Clean mason jar rims and fixes lids and bands correctly.

6. Transfer relish-filled jars to a boiling water canner for processing. Process jars for about ten to

twenty minutes according to your altitude, as described in chapter three.

Apple Chutney

Ingredients

- Sixteen (16) cups of chopped tart apples
- One (1) cup of finely chopped onions
- One (1) cup of red bell peppers, chopped
- Two (2) teaspoons of finely chopped red Serrano pepper
- Twelve (12) ounces of seedless golden raisins
- Four (4) cups of brown sugar
- Three (3) tablespoons of mustard seed

- Two (2) tablespoons of ground ginger

- Two (2) teaspoons of finely ground allspice

- Two (2) teaspoons of canning salt

- One (1) crushed clove of garlic

- Four (4) cups of apple cider vinegar (5%)

Yield: 6 pints

Instructions

1. Under low to medium heat, place washed and sterilized jars and lids in simmering water for heating until time for use. Also, prepare a boiling water canner, and set bands aside.

2. Incorporate all ingredients in a clean saucepan and boil. Reduce heat after a while and simmer for about forty-five minutes until you're pleased with the consistency, stirring as you go.

3. Pour hot chutney into sterile mason jars, ensuring a headspace of half an inch and eliminating any bubbles. Fix lids and bands, then process jars in a boiling water canner for twenty minutes or

according to your altitude, as described in chapter three, and check for seals after twenty-four hours.

Mango Chutney

Ingredients

- Eleven (11) cups of chopped unripe mango

- Two and a half (2½) cups of finely chopped yellow onion

- Two and a half (2½) tablespoons of grated fresh ginger

- One and a half (1½) tablespoons of chopped garlic

- Four and a half (4½) cups of sugar

- Three (3) cups of white vinegar (5%)

- Two and a half (2½) cups of golden raisins

- One and a half (1½) teaspoons of canning salt

- Four (4) teaspoons of chili powder

Yield: 6-pint jars.

Instructions

1. Under low to medium heat, place washed and sterilized jars and lids in simmering water for heating until time for use. Also, prepare a boiling water canner, and set bands aside.

2. Wash fruits properly, cut into cubes, and coarsely puree in a blender. Dice peeled onions, chop garlic, and grate ginger.

3. Combine vinegar and sugar in a stockpot and boil for five minutes. Add the remaining ingredients and boil. Afterward, reduce heat and simmer, making sure to stir properly.

4. Pour hot chutney into mason jars, leaving half an inch headspace. Fix lids and bands properly and

transfer jars to a boiling water canner for processing.

5. Process for about 15-20 minutes based on altitude as given in the altitude adjustments table in chapter 3.

Cranberry Orange Chutney

Ingredients

- Twenty-four (24) ounces of fresh cranberries

- Two (2) cups of chopped white onion

- Two (2) cups of golden raisins

- One and a half (1½) cups of white sugar

- One and a half (1½) cups of packed brown sugar

- Two (2) cups of white distilled vinegar (5%)

- One (1) cup of orange juice

- Four (4) teaspoons of peeled, grated fresh ginger

- Three (3) sticks of cinnamon

Yield: 8 half-pint jars

Instructions

1. Under low to medium heat, place washed and sterilized jars and lids in simmering water for heating until time for use. Also, prepare a boiling water canner, and set bands aside.

2. Rinse cranberries and incorporate all ingredients in a clean dutch oven. Boil mixture over very high heat and reduce heat later on and for fifteen minutes, then discard cinnamon sticks.

3. Pour chutney into hot jars, leaving a headspace of half an inch and removing air bubbles. Fix lids and bands correctly, and process chutney-filled mason jars in a boiling water canner.

4. Process for ten to twenty minutes based on the altitude provided in chapter 3. Remember to check for seals after twenty-four hours.

Lemon Peach Turmeric Chutney

Ingredients

- Three (3) large thinly sliced lemons
- One (1) medium onion, small diced
- Eight to ten (8-10) chopped peaches
- Two (2) red chilis, minced
- Two (2) cloves of garlic, minced
- Two (2) tablespoons of salt

- Two (2) teaspoons of grated fresh ginger

- One and a half (1½) teaspoons of turmeric powder

- Two (2) teaspoons of mustard seeds

- One (1) teaspoon of smoked paprika

- Quarter (¼) cup of bottled lemon juice

- Half (½) cup of cider vinegar

- One (1) cup of sugar

- Quarter (¼) cup of pure honey

Yield: About four (4) pint jars

Instructions

1. Under low to medium heat, place washed and sterilized jars and lids in simmering water for heating until time for use. Also, prepare a boiling water canner, and set bands aside.

2. Incorporate all ingredients in a clean saucepan and boil over very high heat. Lower heat and let the mixture simmer for about thirty minutes until you are happy with the consistency.

3. Fill hot mason jars with hot chutney and ensure a headspace of half an inch. Fix in lids and bands properly and place chutney-filled jars in a boiling water canner for processing.

4. Process for fifteen minutes, taking into consideration your altitude. Check for seals after twenty-four hours.

Orange Rhubarb Chutney

Ingredients

- Ten (10) black peppercorns

- One (1) tablespoon of mustard seeds

- One (1) tablespoon of Ball pickling spice

- Four (4) tablespoons of grated orange zest

- Two-third (2/3) cup of fresh orange juice

- Six (6) cups of chopped rhubarb

- Five (5) cups of brown sugar

- Three and a half (3 ½) cups of cider vinegar

- Three (3) cups of chopped onion

- One and a half (1 ½) cups of raisins

- Two (2) tablespoons of finely chopped garlic

- Two (2) tablespoons of finely chopped ginger roots

- One (1) tablespoon of curry powder

- One (1) teaspoon of finely ground allspice

Yield: About Six (6) half pints

Instructions

1. Under low to medium heat, place washed and sterilized jars and lids in simmering water for heating until time for use. Also, prepare a boiling water canner, and set bands aside.

2. To make a spice bag, bind peppercorns, pickling spice, and mustard seeds in a square of cheesecloth. Place aside.

3. In a sizable stainless-steel saucepan, mix the orange zest and juice, brown sugar, onions, vinegar, rhubarb, raisins, garlic, and ginger. Over medium-high heat, bring to a boil while stirring continuously. Lower the heat and slowly simmer for 45 minutes while you stir periodically.

4. Add the reserved spice bag, curry powder, and allspice. Mix thoroughly. Simmer gently for 30 minutes, stirring often, or until the mixture is sticky enough to tower on a spoon.

5. Fill hot jars with hot chutney, ensuring a headspace of half an inch. Fix lids and bands accurately and transfer jars to a boiling water canner for processing.

6. Process for ten minutes, adjusting for altitudes as described in chapter three, then check for seals after twenty-four hours.

Conclusion

Food preservation exists in diverse forms, but most do not come close to the water bath canning method. This canning method isn't only less expensive to start with and eliminates the action of microorganisms in food but also makes food storage fun and adventurous.

Creative recipes for the water bath canning method, such as pickled vegetables, jams, marmalades, and also relishes, give you the privilege of enjoying fresh food all year round, and with the information shared in the pages of this book, you are on your way to safely preserve your favorite foods for long term storage and consumption.

Happy canning!